Shakesp

Published by Methuen 2003

1 3 5 7 9 10 8 6 4 2

First published in 2003 by
Methuen Publishing Limited,
215 Vauxhall Bridge Road,
London SW1V 1EJ

Methuen Publishing Limited Reg. No. 3543167

A CIP catalogue record for this book is available from the British Library.

ISBN 0 413 77402 3

Typeset by SX Composing
Printed and bound in Great Britain by
Cox and Wyman Ltd, Reading, Berkshire

Caution
All rights in this play are strictly reserved.
Application for performance, etc., should be made before rehearsals begin
to Writers and Artists Agency, 19 West 44th Street, Suite 1410, New York,
New York 10036. No performance may be given unless a licence has
been obtained.

Shakespeare's R & J

an adaptation of

Shakespeare's

Romeo and Juliet

by

Joe Calarco

Methuen Drama

Adapter's note

An all-male *Romeo and Juliet*? The first problem was where to set it. More than anything, I hate a conceptual show that has no concept. If you have a cast made up of men, they better inhabit a world made up of men. The setting of *R & J* is what makes it work. Many people assume that the inspiration for the adaptation came from *Dead Poets Society*. I actually tried to avoid the comparison in order to avoid sentimentality. My inspirations were actually *The Crucible*, where repression leads to psychosis (Romeo's and Juliet's actions are not exactly rational after all), and *Lord of the Flies*, where separation from ordered society leads to primal violence. Both pieces also deal with mob mentality which I think is a strong factor in the energy of *R & J*. *Romeo and Juliet* is in many ways about sexual hysteria. I wanted to fully capture this. The world of *R & J* is a world full of danger. What could be more dangerous than that first forbidden kiss of literature's most famous lovers? The first forbidden kiss of two schoolboys. Put those boys in a school where Catholicism reigns, patriarchy rules, and where simply reading Shakespeare is forbidden, and you have a world pulsating with repressed hysteria.

This is a play about men. It is about how men interact with other men. Thus it deals with how men view women, sex, sexuality, and violence. This play is not *nor should any production of it be* strictly about homoeroticism. Nor should it be strictly about homophobia. These seemed to be the obvious choices when approaching the project, and I purposefully avoided them. Of course these issues exist in the piece. The act of two men kissing is by definition homoerotic, and how can you depict a group of boys acting out a play about romantic love without homophobia rearing its head? However, the thought of seeing a production of this play with a cast of pre-pubescent-looking actors running around the stage half naked or in drag is enough to send me screaming into the night. The goal is simply to tell these boys' story. That is the other key to a successful production. The actors cast are not doing *Romeo and Juliet*. They are

doing *R & J*. Therefore they are playing students first and
foremost, students who are acting out *Romeo and Juliet*. This
is the key to establishing the right tone of the piece, for it
should radiate with a very young, very male, energy. I also
told my actors that I thought the strongest choice was to
make the students heterosexual. To me it makes the
aversion to male romantic love more palpable. It also makes
the students' acceptance of a definition of love without
boundaries more moving and monumental.

The piece is thrilling because it goes to the essence of
pure theatre: just four actors with no set, no costume
changes, and no props, save composition books, a copy of
the play, and a large piece of red fabric. It seemed illogical
for these boys to pull rapiers out from underneath their
'desks'. They must use what they have on hand to create
their play. A piece of fabric that their 'sacred text' is hidden
in seemed a practical 'prop' for them to use. The key is
that it is very practical. It should not be considered abstract.
As long as the actors use the fabric in a very concrete,
practical, way, the audience will accept whatever purpose
it must take on.

To decide to have an all-male cast playing women was by
far the most challenging aspect of the project. The most
rewarding comments I have gotten deal with this gender
issue; many people said that they quickly forgot the one-
gendered nature of the cast and that they never saw the
actors as women or as men playing women. They forgot
about gender altogether. This is the goal. Now ask me how
to achieve that and I would be at a loss. I think basically that
I cast it well. The one thing that I told the actors over and
over is that they were playing a male student first. Once the
students get over their initial embarrassment of playing
women they play the female characters 'straight'. They
never try to become women. We were astonished, though
maybe we shouldn't have been, at how strong these women
are. They were written as powerhouses. Our twentieth-
century view of women has caused us to play them weakly;
they are not written that way. That's the best advice I can
give: just play the character, without physical or emotional

stereotype.

The evening should feel like a communal event. The more you can create the effect that this group of students is a community, or tribe, the more heartbreaking it will be at the end when they realise their 'dream' must end. When the students are not playing a character in the scene being acted out, they are actively watching it, waiting for the next event to happen. This 'watching' adds immeasurably to the energy of the piece; it gives it an urgency that only occurs when people can't wait to see what is going to happen next. The announcements of scenes also add to the energy of the play; it is as if the students are announcing the next game they are going to play.

The preceding notes and following text try to give an impression of the play in production as I directed it and the qualities that I think made those productions work. However, I hope future directors feel free enough to bring their own ideas to the table without going against the intended vision of the piece.

A note on the text

An / sign indicates where the next speaker's lines start as the speech continues.

Shakespeare's R&J received its UK premiere in March 2003 at the Theatre Royal Bath. It was produced by the Splinter Group (Seth A. Goldstein, producer) and Theatre Royal Bath Productions (Danny Moar, producer). The cast was as follows:

Student 1   Matthew Sincell
Student 2   Jason Michael Spelbring
Student 3   Jeremy Beck
Student 4   Jason Dubin

Director Joe Calarco
Lighting design Chris Lee
Scenic design Mike Fagin
Sound design Brian Keating
Costume design Amela Baksic
Assistant director Monica Henderson

The same production subsequently transferred to the Arts Theatre, London on 8 September 2003 with the additional producer Fiery Angel Limited (Edward Snape, producer). The cast also included Daniel Larlham and Dustin Sullivan.

The players

Student 1	Romeo
Student 2	Juliet, Benvolio, Friar John
Student 3	Mercutio, Lady Capulet, Friar Laurence
Student 4	Tybalt, Nurse, Balthasar

Act One

Four **Students** *dressed in slacks, shirts, ties and sweaters, or blazers, march military-like into the space, holding composition books. They kneel as if in chapel and cross themselves.*

All   In the name of the Father, the Son, and the Holy Spirit. Amen. Bless me Father for I have sinned.

Student 2   It has been three days since my last confession . . .

Student 3   It has been two days since my last confession . . .

Student 4   It has been four days since my last confession . . .

Student 2   These are my sins.

Student 3   These are my sins.

Student 4   These are my sins.

Students 2, 3 *and* **4** *whisper confessions under their breath as* **Student 1** *rises and sneaks off. He opens his composition book, thinks and then writes.*

Student 1   My Love, I write and write with no response from you. And I ask myself, 'Can she be so cruel? Does she care at all?' Still, my heart tells me –

He stops writing and scribbles out what he has written. He starts a new letter.

Student 1   My Love, as each day passes without a word or sign from you, I wonder what we –

He again stops and scribbles out what he has written. He searches for the perfect words.

Student 1   My love . . . is as a fever.

He turns the page and frantically begins writing.

My love is as a fever, longing still
For that which longer nurseth the disease,
Feeding on that which doth preserve the ill,
The uncertain sickly appetite to please.
My reason, the physician to my love,
Angry that his prescriptions are not kept,
Hath left me, and I desperate now approve
Desire is death, which physic did except. /
Past cure I am, now reason is past care
And frantic mad with ever more unrest;
My thoughts and my discourse are as madmens are
At random from the truth vainly expressed.
For I have sworn thee fair, and thought thee bright,
Who are as black as hell, as dark as night!

Students 2, 3 and 4
Oh my God, I am heartily sorry
for having offended thee. And I
detest all my sins for thy just
punishments but most of all
because they offend thee my God
who are all good and deserving of
all our love. I firmly resolve with the
help of thy grace to sin no more and
to avoid the occasion of sin. Amen.

School bells ring. The students stand immediately at attention and march off to their first class. They sit.

All (*in unison*) Amo, amas, amat, amamus, amatis, amant.

School bells ring again. The **Students** *again stand at attention and march off to their next class. They sit.*

All (*in unison*) The square of the hypotenuse is equal to the sum of the squares of the remaining sides.

More bells. The **Students** *stand at attention again and march off to their next class. They sit.*

All (*in unison*)   Thou shalt not:

Student 2   Lie!

Student 3   Steal!

Student 4   Cheat!

Student 1   Kill!

All   Lust!

More bells. Again they stand at attention and march to the next class.

Student 1 (*reading from book*)   Let us particularly note the difference in character between the two sexes, a difference so great that one might suppose them members of two different races.

Student 4 (*reading from book*)   It is a woman's responsibility to maintain the comfort and the decency of her family. It is she who makes etiquette, and it is she who preserves the order and the decency of society. Without women, men soon resume the savage state, and the comforts of the home are exchanged for the misery of the mining camp.

Student 3 (*reading from book*)   Whenever you call on a lady, speak of having just come from the club and dwell with pride upon the amount of time you spend there, because all ladies have great faith in the happy influence of such places as clubs upon a young man in not only teaching him the polite accomplishments of chewing and drinking and a great many coarser habits, but they also get him into the pleasant way of late hours, and of spending all of his leisure time away from home. There is no sensible lady who will not jump at the chance of marrying one of these clubmen for she knows that she will be relieved of his company nearly all of the time, and that she will, furthermore, have the great pleasure of sitting up to welcome him home at the poetical hour of midnight. What a charming prospect for domestic happiness.

Student 2 (*reading from book*)   A bold man may disregard and disobey the most sacred laws and customs, but he cannot, he dare not disregard a woman's influence, for the amiable woman rules the haughty man. Hence the business of a man is to govern the world, and the destiny of a woman is to charm and influence it.

All   AMEN.

Bells ring again. After each chime the **Students** *gasp for air. The bells stop. Class is over. They can breathe again. They sit. Bells chime one more time.* **Students 2**, **3** *and* **4** *snap to attention.*

Students 2, 3 and 4   Now I lay me down to sleep, I pray the Lord my soul to keep, and if I die before I wake, I pray the Lord my soul . . . (*They fall asleep as the campus goes to 'lights out'.*)

Student 1 *sneaks out of his bed. He awakens* **Students 2** *and* **3**.)

Student 1 (*whispering*)   Now it is the time of night . . .

Student 1 *grabs a flashlight and the three set off. They hear a sound and the beam hits* **Student 4** *in the face, waking him.* **Students 1**, **2** *and* **3** *go to him.*

Student 1   Now it is the time of night.
   That the graves, all gaping wide,
   Every one lets forth his sprite,
   In the churchway paths to glide;

Student 1 *collects the composition books and puts them aside.*
   And we fairies, that do run
   By the triple Hecate's team

Student 1 *tries to lift up one of the floor boards. It is heavy.*
Student 3 *helps him.*

   From the presence of the sun,
   Following darkness like a dream . . .

Student 1 *lifts an object from beneath the floorboards wrapped in a vibrant swathe of red fabric. He unwraps it.*

Now . . . are . . . frolic.

The other boys' flashlight beams hit the book's cover, revealing it is a copy of Romeo and Juliet. *They fall back excited and scared. Moonlight streams magically into the dark room. The boys lunge for the book and then look around, terrified of being caught.*

Student 1   I dreamt a dream tonight.

Student 1 *huddles in the corner.* **Students 2**, **3** *and* **4** *gather around to listen.* **Student 1** *slowly opens the mysterious book. It is a magical moment. The other boys wait anxiously, desperate to hear the contents, yet terrified of getting caught.* **Student 1** *finally reads.*

Two households both alike in dignity
(In fair Verona, where we lay our scene)
From ancient grudge break to new mutiny,
Where civil blood makes civil hands unclean.
From forth the fatal loins of these two foes
A pair of star-cross'd lovers take their life,
Whose misadventur'd piteous overthrows
Doth with their death bury their parents' strife.
The fearful passage of their death-mark'd love
And the continuance of their parents' rage,
Which, but their children's end, nought could remove,
Is now the two hours' to traffic of our stage;
The which, if you with patient ears attend,
What here shall miss, our toil shall strive to mend.

Student *1* *offers the book to the others, daring them to read from it.* **Student 2** *accepts the dare and runs and grabs the book.*

Student 2   Draw thy tool. (*Giggles all around.*) Here comes two of the house of Montagues.

Student 2 *offers up the book.* **Student 3** *accepts the dare and grabs it.*

Student 3   My naked weapon is out.

Student 3 *offers up the book.* **Student 4** *accepts the dare and grabs the book.*

Student 4   A dog of that house shall move me to stand. I will take the wall of any man or maid of Montague's.

Student 4 *hands the book to* **Student 2**.

Student 2   The weakest goes to the wall, and therefore women, being the weaker vessels, are ever thrust to the wall.

As the relay continues, the boys get more and more excited. **Student 2** *throws the book to* **Student 1**.

Student 1   Therefore I will push Montague's men from the wall, and thrust his maids to the wall.

Student 3 *runs and grabs the book from* **Student 1**.

Student 3   I will show myself a tyrant: when I have fought with the men I will be cruel with the maids, I will cut off their heads.

Student 2 *runs and grabs the book from* **Student 3**.

Student 2   Me they shall feel while I am able to stand, and 'tis known I am a pretty piece of flesh.

Student 4 *grabs the book from* **Student 2** *and sees the next tantalising stage direction and reads it aloud.*

Student 4   They duel.

Rabid with excitement, the boys clear the space to get ready for the duel. They realise they have no weapons to fight with. **Student 4** *has an idea and picks up the long piece of red fabric. He hands one end to* **Student 1** *and the other to* **Student 3**. **Student 4** *grabs the center of the fabric.* **Student 2** *holds up the book for him to read from.*

Student 4   Quarrel, I will back thee.

Student 4 *lets go of the fabric and* **Students 1** *and* **3** *begin a fierce tug-of-war. Student 1 is winning so* **Student 2** *runs and joins with* **Student 3**, *so* **Student 4** *quickly joins* **Student 1**. *The boys are having a great time with this battle. Eventually only* **Student 2** *and* **Student 4** *are left to battle it out, the others having fallen off.* **Student 2** *is eventually victorious, pulling* **Student 4** *to the ground. As the other three celebrate the victory,* **Student 4** *slowly stands and turns to* **Student 2**.

Student 4 (*as Tybalt*)   Turn thee! . . . Benvolio. (**Student 2** *turns to him. Things are serious now.*) Look upon thy death.

They square off. **Students 1** *and* **3** *begin drumming an iambic pentameter rhythm.* **Students 2** *and* **4** *pull the fabric taut and begin to circle to the metered tempo. As they turn they chant in meter.*

All   The fearful passage of their death-mark'd love
Is now the two hours' traffic of our stage.
The fearful passage of their death-mark'd love
Is now the two hours' traffic of our stage.
The fearful passage of their death-mark'd love
IS NOW THE TWO HOURS' TRAFFIC OF OUR
STAGE!

We are suddenly thrust into the reality of Romeo and Juliet.

Student 2   VILLAIN!

Students 2 *and* **4** *engage in a fierce duel.* **Students 1** *and* **3** *drum a wild percussive accompaniment. As* **Student 2** *strikes the final blow,* **Student 4** *dies. Pause. Then* **Student 4** *laughs and the rest join in, enjoying the game and this taste of freedom.* **Student 3** *grabs the book and reads the next section grandly.*

Student 3 (*as Lord Mantague*)
O where is Romeo, saw you him today?
Right glad I am he was not at this fray.

He passes the book off to **Student 2** *who reads.*

Student 2 (*as Benvolio*)
Uncle, an hour before the worshipp'd sun
Peer'd forth the golden window of the east
A troubled mind drove me to walk abroad . . .

He peers at **Student 1** *and gets an idea. He picks up* **Student 1**'s *composition book and a pencil.*

Where underneath the grove of sycamore
That westward rooteth from the city's side

He hands the composition book and pencil to **Student 1**.

So early walking did I see your son.

Student 2 *pushes* **Student 1** *centre stage.* **Student 1** *writes furiously in his composition book.*

Student 1 (*as Romeo*)
　　Love is a smoke made with the fume of sighs;
　　Being purg'd, a fire sparkling in lovers' eyes;
　　Being vex'd, a sea nourish'd with lovers' tears;
　　What is it else?

Student 4 *grabs the book from him, sits on him so he cannot move and reads from the composition book, laughing.*

Student 2　'A madness most discreet,
　　A choking gall, and a preserving sweet.'

He calls the other two boys over. They grab the composition book and read from it, laughing over its contents.

Student 4　'Many a morning hath he there been seen,
　　With tears augmenting the fresh morning dew.'

Student 3　'Adding to clouds more clouds with his deep sighs;'

Student 4　'Away from the light steals home our heavy friend'

Student 3　'And private in his chamber pens himself,'

Student 4　Shuts up his windows,

Student 3　　　　　　　　　　　　– locks fair daylight out

Student 4　And makes himself an artificial night.

Student 2　Come my good friends, speak, do you know the cause?

Student 1 *breaks free and grabs his composition book.*

Student 1 (*as Romeo*)　In sadness cousin –

He holds his hand out to **Student 2** *who grabs it and takes on the role of Benvolio.*

　　　　　　　　　　　　　　I do love a woman.

All the boys revel at this news. **Students 1** *and* **2** *whisper secretly.*

Student 2 (*as Benvolio*)
  I aim'd so near when I suppos'd you lov'd.

Student 1 (*as Romeo*)
  A right good markman; and she's fair I love.

Student 2 (*as Benvolio*)
  A right fair mark, fair coz, is soonest hit.

Student 1 (*as Romeo*)
  Well, in that hit you miss; she'll not be hit
  With Cupid's arrow, she hath Dian's wit,
  And, in strong proof of chastity well arm'd,
  From love's weak childish bow she lives uncharm'd.
  She will not stay the siege of loving terms,
  Nor bide th'encounter of assailing eyes
  Nor ope her lap to saint-seducing gold;
  O she is rich in beauty, only poor,
  That when she dies, with beauty dies her store.

Student 2 (*as Benvolio*)
  Then she hath sworn that she will still live chaste?

Student 1 (*as Romeo*)
  She hath, and in that sparing makes huge waste.
  For beauty starv'd with her severity
  Cuts beauty off from all posterity.
  She is too fair, too wise, wisely too fair,
  To merit bliss by making me despair.
  She hath forsworn to love, and in that vow
  Do I live dead, that live to tell it now.

Student 2 (*as Benvolio*)
  Be rul'd by me, forget to think of her.

Student 1 (*as Romeo*)
  O teach me how I should forget to think.

Student 2 (*as Benvolio*)
  By giving liberty unto thine eyes:
  Examine other beauties.

This night at Capulet's once yearly feast.
Sups the fair ROSALINE –

Knowing he has revealed a secret, **Student 2** *makes a run for it.*
Student 1 *chases after him.*

                       – whom thou so lovest,
With all the admired beauties of Verona.
Go thither and with unattainted eye
Compare her face with some that I shall show
And I will make thee think thy swan a crow.

Student 1 *tackles* **Student 2** *and clamps his own hand over*
Student 2*'s mouth.*

Student 1 (*as Romeo*)
When the devout religion of mine eye
Maintains such falsehood, then turn tears to fires,
And these, who often drown'd, could never die,
Transparent heretics, be burnt for liars!
One fairer than my love! The all-seeing sun
Ne'er saw her match since first the world begun.

Student 2 (*as Benvolio*)
Tut, you saw her fair, none else being by:
Herself pois'd with herself in either eye.
But in that crystal scales let there be weigh'd
Your lady's love against some other maid
That I will show you shining at this feast,
And she shall scant show well that now seems best.

Student 1 (*as Romeo*)
I'll go along, no such sight to be shown,
But to rejoice in splendour of mine own.

The boys whoop and cheer. **Students 2**, **3**, *and* **4** *slam against each*
other as **Student 1** *grabs the book and reads.*

Student 1 (*as Romeo*)
Give me a torch, I am not for this ambling.
Being but heavy I will bear the light.

Student 4   Come my good friend, now we must have you dance.

Student 4 grabs Student 1 and begins to dance with him. The others laugh. Student 1 breaks away, trying to go on with the play.

Student 1 (*as Romeo*)   Not I!

He closes his eyes puts his finger out to point and circles around. When he stops and opens his eyes, he is pointing at Student 3.

You (*He throws the script to Student 3.*) Mercutio –

This casting announcement earns cheers and applause from the other boys.

– have dancing shoes
With nimble soles, I have a soul of lead
So stakes me to the ground I cannot move.

Student 3 *reads his part from the script.*

Student 3 (*as Mercutio*)
You are a lover, borrow Cupid's wings
And soar with them above a common bound.

Students 2 *and* **4** *grab* **Student 1** *by the hands and feet and start swinging him around in the air.* **Student 1** *struggles to get away.*

Student 1 (*as Romeo*)
I am too sore enpierced with his shaft
To soar with his light feathers, and so bound
I cannot bound a pitch above dull woe.

Student 1 *breaks free.*
Under love's heavy burden do I sink.

Student 3 *drops the script and continues on with his part.*

Student 3 (*as Mercutio*)
And, to sink in it, should you burden love
Too great oppression for a tender thing.

They start wrestling.

Student 1 (*as Romeo*)
   Is love a tender thing? It is too rough,
   Too rude, too boisterous, and it pricks like thorn.

Student 3 (*as Mercutio*)
   If love be rough with you, be rough with love;
   Prick love for pricking and you beat love down.

Come, we burn daylight, ho!

Students 2 *and* **4** *grab* **Student 1** *and begin to pull him off to the ball.*

Student 1 (*as Romeo*)   Nay, that's not so.

Student 3 (*as Mercutio*)   I mean sir, in delay
   We waste our lights in vain, like lamps by day.
   Take our good meaning, for our judgement sits
   Five times in that ere once in our five wits.

Student 1 (*as Romeo*)
And we mean well in going to this mask,
But tis no wit to go.

Student 3 (*as Mercutio*)   Why, may one ask?

Student 1 *breaks free, grabs the script, and runs to* **Student 3**.

Student 1 (*as Romeo*)
   I dreamt a dream tonight!

Student 3 (*as Mercutio*)
                     And so did I.

Student 1 (*as Romeo*)
   Well what was yours?

Student 3 (*as Mercutio*)
                That dreamers often lie.

Student 3 *pushes* **Student 1** *to the ground.*

Student 1 (*as Romeo*)
In bed asleep, while they do dream things true.

Student 3 (*as Mercutio*)
    O then I see Queen Mab hath been with you.

Students *gather around to listen to the story.* **Student 3** *grabs the script and reads from it.*

    She is the fairies' midwife, and she comes
    In shape no bigger than an agate stone
    On the forefinger of an alderman,
    Drawn with a team of little atomies
    Over men's noses as they lie asleep.
    Her chariot is an empty hazelnut
    Made by the joiner squirrel or old grub,
    Time out o' mind the fairies' coachmakers;
    Her waggon-spokes made of long spiders' legs,
    The cover of the wings of grasshoppers,
    The traces of the smallest spider web,
    The collars of the moonshine's watery beams,
    Her whip of cricket's bone, the lash of film,
    Her wagoner a small grey-coated gnat,
    Not half so big as a round little worm
    Prick'd from the lazy finger of a maid;

Student 3 *drops the script and gallops about. They others follow, laughing.*

    And in this state she gallops night by night
    Through lovers' brains, and then they dream of love;
    Oe'r ladies' lips, who straight on kisses dream,
    Which oft the angry Mab with blisters plagues
    Because their breaths with sweetmeats tainted are.

Student 3 *grabs* **Student 1**, *dips him, and kisses him. The others laugh and begin taunting him with the old childhood song —*

Student 3   '. . . sitting in a tree. K-I-S-S-I-N-G. First comes love, then comes marriage, then comes junior in the baby carriage . . .

Student 3 *tries to make a run for it but the boys block his way and make kissing sounds.*

Student 3   Sometime she driveth o'er a soldier's neck
And then dreams he of cutting foreign throats,
Of breaches, ambuscadoes, Spanish blades,
Of healths five fathom deep; and then anon
Drums in his ear, at which he starts and wakes,
And being thus frighted swears a prayer or two
And sleeps again. This is that very Mab
That plaits the manes of horses in the night
And bakes the elf-locks in foul sluttish hairs,
Which, once untangled, much misfortune bodes.

Students 2 and **3** *begin stalking him and doing the k-i-s-s-i-n-g taunt again.*

This is the hag, when maids lie on their backs,
That presses them and learns them first to bear,
Making them women of good carriage.
This is she – . . . !

Trying to escape the taunting, **Student 3** *makes a run for it.*
Student 1 *grabs him and tries to calm him.*

Student 1 (*as Romeo*)   Peace, peace, Mercutio, peace!
Thou talk'st of nothing.

He holds out his hand to **Student 3** *who takes it.*

Student 3 (*as Mercutio*)   True, I talk of dreams,
Which are the children of an idle brain,
Begot of nothing but vain fantasy,
Which is as thin of substance as the air
And more inconstant than the wind, who woos
Even now the frozen bosom of the north
And, being anger'd, puffs away from thence
Turning his face to the dew-dropping south.

Students 2 and **4** *approach, attempting an apology.*

Student 2   This wind you talk of blows us from
ourselves . . .

Student 4   Strike, drum?

He offers his hand to **Student 3** *who grabs it and jumps up and begins drumming and chanting with* **Students 2** *and* **4** *until* **Student 1** *silences them by whipping the cloth. He backs away.*

Student 1 (*announces*)   Juliet's bedchamber.

Students 2, 3 *and* **4** *set up* **Juliet**'s *bedroom.*

Student 3   Enter Lady Capulet.

Student 3 *strikes a very stereotypical 'feminine' pose.*

Student 4   Enter Nurse.

(**Student 4** *strikes a very stereotypical 'feminine' pose.*)

Student 3   Nurse, where's my daughter?

He strikes another pose.

Call her forth to me.

Student 4 *strikes another pose.*

Student 4   Now, by my maidenhead, at twelve year old, I bade her come.

Students 3 *and* **4** *are getting sillier and sillier with their 'playing' of women. Meanwhile,* **Student 1** *has given* **Student 2** *the red piece of fabric which transforms him into* **Juliet**.)

Student 3   Juliet?!

Student 4   What, lamb! What, ladybird!

Student 3   Juliet?!

Student 4   God forbid. Where's this girl?

Student 3   Juliet!!

Student 4   What, Juliet!

They laugh. **Student 1** *'enters' as* **Juliet**. *This is not a game to him.*

Student 2 (*as Juliet*)   How now, who calls?

Students 2 *and* **3** *stop laughing.*

Student 4   Your mother.

Student 2 *sits and spreads the fabric out like a wide skirt or quilt.*
Student 3, *as* **Lady Capulet**, *and* **Student 4**, *as the*
Nurse, *join him and sit with the cloth on their laps and all three*
begin to simulate sewing.

Student 2 (*as Juliet*)   Madam, I am here, what is your will?

Student 3 (*as Lady Capulet*)   This is the matter. Nurse, give
leave awhile,
   We must talk in secret.

Student 4 *leaves and joins* **Student 1** *to watch the scene.*
Student 3 *attempts to talk to* **Student 2**. *It is difficult.*

                              Nurse, come back again,
   I have remember'd me.

Student 4 *rejoins the scene as the* **Nurse**.

                              Thou's hear our counsel.
   Thou know'st my daughter's of a pretty age.

Student 4 (*as Nurse*)
   Faith, I can tell her age unto an hour.

Student 3 (*as Lady Capulet*)

                              She's not fourteen.

Student 4 (*as Nurse*)
   I'll lay fourteen of my teeth –
   And yet, to my teen be it spoken, I have but four –
   She's not fourteen. How long is it now
   To Lammas-tide?

Student 3 (*as Lady Capulet*)
   A fortnight and odd days.

Student 4 (*as Nurse*)
   Even or odd, of all days in the year,
   Come Lammas Eve at night shall she be fourteen.
   Susan and she – God rest all Christian souls –
   Were of an age. Well, Susan is with God;

She was too good for me. But as I said,
On Lammas Eve at night shall she be fourteen.
That shall she;

(*Pause.* **Student 3** *is about to address* **Student 2** *again.*)

     Marry, I remember it well.
Tis since the earthquake now eleven years,
And she was wean'd – I never shall forget it –
Of all the days of the year upon that day.
And since that time it is eleven years,
For then she could stand high-lone, nay, by the rood,
She could have run and waddled all about;
For even the day before she broke her brow,
And then my husband – God be with his soul,
He was a merry man – took up the child,
'Yea', quoth he, 'dost thou fall upon thy face?
Thou wilt fall backward when thou hast more wit,
Wilt thou not, Jule?' And by my holidame,
The pretty wretch left crying and said 'Ay'.
To see now how a jest shall come about!
I warrant, and I should live a thousand years
I never should forget it. 'Wilt thou not, Jule?' quoth he,
And, pretty fool, it stinted, and said 'Ay.'

Student 3 (*as Lady Capulet*)
Enough of this, I pray thee, hold thy peace!

Student 4 (*as Nurse*)
Yes, madam . . .

Student 3 *is about to continue.*

     Yet I cannot choose but laugh
To think it should leave crying and say 'Ay';
And yet I warrant it had upon its brow
A bump as big as a young cock'rel's stone,
A perilous knock, and it cried bitterly.
'Yea', quoth my husband, 'fall'st upon thy face?
Thou wilt fall backward when thou com'st to age,
Wilt thou not, Jule?' It stinted, and said 'Ay'.

Student 2 (*as Juliet*)
> And stint thou too, I pray thee, Nurse, say I.

Student 4 (*as Nurse*)
> Peace, I have done. God mark thee to his grace,
> Thou wast the prettiest babe that e'er I nurs'd.
> And I might live to see thee married once,
> I have my wish.

Student 3 (*as Lady Capulet*)
> Marry, that marry is the very theme
> I came to talk of. Tell me, daughter Juliet,
> How stands your disposition to be married?

Student 2 (*as Juliet*)
> It is an honor that I dream not of.

Student 4 (*as Nurse*)
> An honour. Were not I thine only nurse
> I would say thou hadst suck'd wisdom from thy teat.

Student 3 (*as Lady Capulet*)
> Well, think of marriage now. Younger than you
> Here in Verona, ladies of esteem,
> Are made already mothers. By my count
> I was your mother much upon these years
> That you are now a maid. Thus then in brief:
> The valiant Paris seeks you for his love.

Student 4 (*as Nurse*)
> A man, young lady. Lady, such a man
> As all the world – why, he's a man of wax.

Student 3 (*as Lady Capulet*)
> Verona's summer hath not such a flower.

Student 4 (*as Nurse*)
> Nay, he's a flower, in faith a very flower.

Student 3 (*as Lady Capulet*)
> What say you, can you love the gentleman?
> This night you shall behold him at our feast;
> Read o'er the volume of your Paris' face

And find delight writ there with beauty's pen.
Examine every married lineament.
Speak briefly, can you like of Paris' love?

Student 2 (*as Juliet*)
I'll look to like, if looking liking move,
But no more deep will I endart mine eye
Than your consent gives strength to make it fly.

Student 1 *enters as a* **Servant**.

Student 1 (*as Servant*)   Madam, the guests are come,
supper served up, you called, my young lady asked for, the
Nurse cursed in the pantry, and everything in extremity. I
must hence to wait, I beseech you follow straight.

He exits the scene.

Student 3 (*as Lady Capulet*)
We follow thee; Juliet, the County stays.

He exits the scene.

Student 4 (*as Nurse*)
Go, girl, seek happy nights to happy days.

*Suddenly, magically, Elizabethan music starts playing. The boys are
mesmerised and then excited as they realise what is coming next.*

All   The ball.

*The boys grab each other playfully and dance foolishly in a teenage
way, switching partners as they go. Eventually* **Student 3**'s *and*
Student 4's *dancing turns into horseplay and then wrestling.
During the last switch of partners,* **Student 1** *is left dancing with*
Student 2. *Their dancing becomes intimate.*

Student 1 (*as Romeo*)
Did my heart love till now? Foreswear it sight.
For I ne'er saw true beauty till this night.

They dance awkwardly cheek to cheek. **Students 3** *and* **4** *notice this
intimacy.* **Student 4** *takes on the role of Tybalt.*

Student 4 (*as Tybalt*)
 This by his voice should be a Montague.
 What, dares the slave
 Come hither, cover'd with an antic face,
 To fleer and scorn at our solemnity?
 Now by the stock and honour of my kin,
 To strike him dead I hold it not a sin.

Student 4 *makes a go at* **Students 1** *and* **2** *who quickly break apart.* **Student 2** *goes and leans against a wall.*

Student 4 (*as Tybalt*)
 I will withdraw; but this intrusion shall
 Now seeming sweet, convert to bitter'st gall.

Students 3 *and* **4** *lean against the wall as if at a school dance not watching the scene.* **Student 1** *sneaks over to* **Student 2** *and grabs his hand.* **Student 2** *tries to pull away.*

Student 1 (*as Romeo*)
 If I profane with my unworthiest hand
 This holy shrine, the gentle sin is this:
 My lips, two blushing pilgrims, ready stand
 To smooth that rough touch with a tender kiss.

Student 1 *kisses* **Student 2**'s *hand.* **Student 2** *pulls away. Despondent,* **Student 1** *starts to exit.* **Student 2** *stops him.*

Student 2 (*as Juliet*)   Gentle pilgrim!!

Students 3 *and* **4** *turn and glare, suspiciously.* **Student 2** *throws his arm over* **Student 1**'s *shoulder in a manly, 'buddy,' sort of way and walks him to sit down side by side.* **Students 3** *and* **4** *look on disapprovingly.* **Students 1** *and* **2** *turn and face away from each other to make it appear as if they are not talking to one another.* **Students 3** *and* **4** *back off.*

Student 2 (*as Juliet*)   You do wrong your hand too much,
  Which mannerly devotion shows in this;

Student 2 *places his hand on* **Student 1**'s *leg.* **Student 1** *places his hand on* **Student 2**'s *hand.*
 For saints have hands that pilgrims' hands do touch,

And palm to palm is holy palmers' kiss.

Student 1 (*as Romeo*)
Have not saints lips, and holy palmers too?

Student 2 (*as Juliet*)
Ay, pilgrim, lips that they must use in prayer.

Student 1 (*as Romeo*)
O then, dear saint, let lips do what hands do:
They pray: grant thou, lest faith turn to despair.

Student 2 (*as Juliet*)
Saints do not move, though grant for prayer's sake.

Student 1 (*as Romeo*)
Then move not, while my prayer's effect I take.

They go to kiss, but it is difficult for it is a moment filled with terror and excitement. Eventually their lips meet. Nothing will ever be the same. **Students 3** *and* **4** *watch in shock.* **Students 1** *and* **2**, *fearful of being caught, manage to break apart.*

Student 1 (*as Romeo*)
Thus from my lips, by thine, my sin is purg'd.

Student 2 (*as Juliet*)
Then have my lips the sin that they have took.

Student 1 (*as Romeo*)
Sin from my lips? O trespass sweetly urg'd.
Give me my sin again.

They kiss again passionately. **Students 3** *and* **4** *notice.*

Student 4 (*aghast, breaks in*)   MADAM!

Terrified, **Students 1** *and* **2** *stand at attention and recite in unison.*

Students 1 and 2   Amo, amas, amat, amamus, amatis, amant.

Student 4 *throws* **Student 1** *centre stage and circles him, ridiculing him.*

Student 4   My friends, this is a . . . Montague our foe
A villain that is hither come in spite
To scorn at our solemnity this night.
I'll not endure him.

He goes to attack **Student 1** *but is stopped by* **Student 2** *who pleads with him.*

Student 2   Enter Nurse.

Student 4 *acquiesces.*

Student 4 (*as Nurse*)   Madam, your mother craves a word with you.

Student 3 *approaches* **Student 2** *as* **Lady Capulet**.
Student 1 *approaches* **Student 4**.

Student 1 (*as Romeo*)   What is her mother?

Student 4 (*as Nurse*)   Marry bachelor,
Her mother is the lady of the house,
And a good lady, and a wise and virtuous.
I nurs'd her daughter that you talk'd withal.
I tell you, he that can lay hold of her
Shall have the chinks.

Student 1 (*as Romeo*)   Is she a Capulet?
O dear account. My life is my foe's debt.

Student 2 (*as Juliet*)   Come hither Nurse.

Student 1 *grabs* **Student 3** *who takes on the role of* **Mercutio**.

Student 1 (*as Romeo*)   Mercutio!

Student 2 (*as Juliet*)   What's he that follows there, that would not dance?

Student 4 (*as Nurse*)   I know not.

Student 2 (*as Juliet*)   Go ask his name.

Student 1 *breaks away from* **Student 3** *and runs out of the ball.*

Student 3 (*as Mercutio*)   Romeo?!

Student 2 (*as Juliet*)   If he be married,
My grave is like to be my wedding bed.

Student 4 (*as Nurse*)   His name is Romeo –

Student 3 (*as Mercutio*) (*in unison with* **Student 4***'s 'Romeo'*)
Romeo?!!

Student 4 (*as Nurse*)   – and a Montague,
The only son of your great enemy.

Student 2 (*as Juliet*)
My only love sprung from my only hate.
Too early seen unknown, and known too late.
Prodigious birth of love it is to me
That I must love a loathed enemy.

Student 4 (*as Nurse*)   What's this? What's this?

Student 2 (*as Juliet*)   A rhyme I learn'd even now
Of one I danc'd withal.

Student 4 (*as Nurse*)   Anon, anon!
Come let's away, the strangers all are gone.

They begin to exit.

Student 4 (*suddenly*)   Act 2 Scene 1. Benvolio and
Mercutio search for Romeo.

Student 2 (*as Benvolio*) *peers over the orchard wall while*
Student 3 (*as Mercutio*) *sits to the side, despondent.*

Student 2 (*as Benvolio*)   Romeo . . . My cousin Romeo . . .
Romeo . . .

Student 3 (*as Mercutio*)   He is wise,
And on my life hath stol'n him home to bed.

Student 2 (*as Benvolio*)
He ran this way and leapt this orchard wall.
Romeo!

He goes to his friend and tries to get him to help.

Call good Mercutio.

Student 3 (*as Mercutio*)   Nay, I'll conjure too:
Romeo . . . Humours . . . Madman . . . Passion . . .
LOVER!

Student 2, *concerned that* **Student 3***'s yelling will get them caught, pulls him down from the wall.*

Appear thou in the likeness of a sigh,
Speak but one rhyme and I am satisfied.
Cry but ay me! Pronounce but love and dove –

Student 2 *clamps his hand over* **Student 3***'s mouth to shut him up, which he does.*

He heareth not, he stirreth not, he moveth not:
The ape is dead and I must conjure him.
I conjure thee by Rosaline's bright eyes,
By her high forehead and her scarlet lip,
By her fine foot, straight leg, and quivering THIGH!

Student 3 *makes a run for the top of the wall again.*

Student 2 (*as Benvolio*)
And if he hear thee, thou wilt anger him.

Student 2 *pulls* **Student 3** *down again.*

Student 3 (*as Mercutio*)
This cannot anger him. My invocation
Is fair and honest; in his mistress' name
I conjure only but to raise up him.

Student 2 (*as Benvolio*)
Come, he hath hid himself among these trees
To be consorted with the humorous night.
Blind is his love, and best befits the dark.

Student 3 (*as Mercutio*)   If love be blind, love cannot hit
the mark.

Student 2 *exits the scene.* **Student 3** *peers over the wall.*

O Romeo, that she were – O that she were –

Romeo, good night. I'll to my truckle bed.
This field bed is too cold for me to sleep.

There is a clap of thunder. Then another. It begins to rain. The **Students** *luxuriate in it. More thunder and lightning – the power goes out, plunging the room into darkness.* **Student 1** *notices the script and picks it up. He grabs a flashlight and begins reading.*

Student 1 (*as Romeo*)   Act 2 Scene 2. A balcony.

Students 3 *and* **4** *grab flashlights and gather around* **Student 1**, *reading over his shoulder.*

But soft, what light through yonder window breaks?
It is the east and Juliet is the sun!

Student 1 *rises as* **Juliet**.
Arise fair sun and kill the envious moon
Who is already sick and pale with grief
That thou her maid art far more fair than she.
Be not her maid since she is envious,
Her vestal livery is but sick and green
And none but fools do wear it. Cast it off!

Student 2 (*as Juliet*)   O Romeo . . .

Student 1 *illuminates* **Student 2** *with the flashlight. The rest of the scene is lit by prowling flashlights.*

Student 1 (*as Romeo*)   It is my lady, O it is my love.
O that she knew she were.

Student 2 (*as Juliet*)   Romeo . . .

Student 1 (*as Romeo*)
She speaks, yet she says nothing. What of that?
Her eye discourses, I will answer it.
I am too bold. 'Tis not to me she speaks.
Two of the fairest stars in all the heaven,
Having some business, do entreat her eyes
To twinkle in their spheres till they return.
What if her eyes were there, they in her head?
The brightness of her cheek would shame those stars

As daylight doth a lamp. Her eyes in heaven
Would through the airy region stream so bright
That birds would sing and think it were not night.
See how she leans her cheek upon her hand.
O that I were a glove upon that hand,
That I might touch that cheek.

Student 2 (*as Juliet*)   Wherefore art thou Romeo?
Deny thy father and refuse thy name.
Or if thou wilt not, be but sworn my love
And I'll no longer be a Capulet.

Student 1 (*as Romeo*)
She speaks.
O speak again bright angel, for thou art
As glorious to this night, being o'er my head,
As is a winged messenger of heaven
Unto the white-upturned wondering eyes
Of mortals that fall back to gaze on him
When he bestrides the lazy-pacing clouds
And sails upon the bosom of the air.

Student 2 (*as Juliet*)
Tis but thy name that is my enemy:
Thou art thyself, though not a Montague.
What's Montague? It is nor hand nor foot
Nor arm nor face nor any other part
Belonging to a man. O be some other name.
What's in a name? That which we call a rose
By any other name would smell as sweet;
So Romeo would, were he not Romeo call'd,
Retain that dear perfection which he owes
Without that title. Romeo, doff thy name,
And for thy name, which is no part of thee,
Take all myself!

Student 1 (*as Romeo*)   I take thee at thy word!
Call me but love, and I'll be new baptis'd:
Henceforth I never will be Romeo.

Students 2, **3** *and* **4** *search for the source of the voice with their* *flashlights.*

Student 2 (*as Juliet*)
    What man art thou that thus bescreen'd in night
    So stumblest on my counsel?

Student 1 (*as Romeo*)   By a name
    I know not how to tell thee who I am:
    My name, dear saint, is hateful to myself
    Because it is an enemy to thee.
    Had I it written, I would tear the word.

Student 2 (*as Juliet*)
    My ears have yet not drunk a hundred words
    Of thy tongue's uttering, yet I know the sound.
    Art thou not Romeo, and a Montague?

The flashlights of **Students 2**, **3**, *and* **4** *hit* **Student 1**.

Student 1 (*as Romeo*)
    Neither, fair saint, if either thee dislike.

Students 3 *and* **4** *descend on* **Student 2**, *unhappy with the way* *this scene is going.*

Student 2 (*as Juliet*)
    How cam'st thou hither, tell me, and wherefore?
    The orchard walls are high and hard to climb,
    And the place death, considering who thou art,
    If any of my kinsmen find thee here.

Student 1 *runs to* **Student 2** *and drags him from the other boys.* **Students 3** *and* **4** *try to pull them apart.*

Student 1 (*as Romeo*)
    With love's light wings did I o'erperch these walls,
    For stony limits cannot hold love out,
    And what love can do, that dares love attempt:
    Therefore thy kinsmen are no stop to me.

Student 2 (*as Juliet*)
    If they do see thee, they will murder thee.

Student 1 (*as Romeo*)
  Alack, there lies more peril in thine eye
  Than twenty of their swords. Look thou but sweet
  And I am proof against their enmity.

Student 1 *manages to pull away. He backs off, as does*
Student 2. **Student 1** *lies down on the floor.*

Student 1   Now I lay me down to sleep . . .

Student 2 *lies down on the other side of the room.*

Student 1 and 2   I pray the Lord my soul to keep.

Students 3 *and* **4** *also go to lie down.*

All   And if I die before I wake. I pray the Lord my soul to
take.

Student 3 *takes one more look up, shining his light on* **Students
1** *and* **2**, *making sure they are asleep. Then he himself goes to sleep.
After a moment,* **Student 1** *gets up and turns his flashlight on,
shining it on* **Student 2** *who tries to stop him from approaching.*

Student 2 (*as Juliet*)
  I would not for the world they saw thee here.

Student 1 (*as Romeo*)
  I have night's cloak to hide me from their eyes,
  And but thou love me, let them find me here.
  My life were better ended by their hate
  Than death prorogued, wanting of thy love.

Student 1 *runs to* **Student 2** *and jumps on him, and kisses him.
As they spin around a huge moon and stars appear. They are in awe of
and delighted by this new environment.*

Student 2 (*as Juliet*)
  By whose direction found'st thou out this place?

Student 1 (*as Romeo*)
  By love, that first did prompt me to enquire.
  He lent me counsel, and I lent him eyes.
  I am no pilot, yet wert thou as far

As that vast shore wash'd with the farthest sea
I should adventure for such merchandise.

Student 2 (*as Juliet*)
Thou know'st the mask of night is on my face,
Else would a maiden blush bepaint my cheek
For that which thou hast heard me speak tonight.
Fain would I dwell on form; fain, fain deny
What I have spoke. But farewell, compliment.
Dost thou love me? I know thou wilt say 'Ay',
And I will take thy word. Yet, if thou swear'st,
Thou mayst prove false. At lovers' perjuries,
They say Jove laughs. O gentle Romeo,
If thou dost love, pronounce it faithfully.
Or, if thou think'st I am too quickly won,
I'll frown and be perverse and say thee nay,
So thou wilt woo; but else, not for the world.
In truth, fair Montague, I am too fond,
And therefore thou mayst think my haviour light,
But trust me, gentleman, I'll prove more true
Than those that have more cunning to be strange.
I should have been more strange, I must confess,
But that thou overheard'st, ere I was ware,
My true love's passion; therefore pardon me,
And not impute this yielding to light love
Which the dark night hath so discovered.

Student 1 (*as Romeo*)
Lady, by yonder blessed moon I vow,
. That tips with silver all these fruit-tree tops –

Student 2 (*as Juliet*)
O swear not by the moon, th'inconstant moon,
That monthly changes in her circled orb,
Lest that thy love prove likewise variable.

Student 1 (*as Romeo*)
What shall I swear by?

Student 2 (*as Juliet*)   Do not swear at all.
Or if thou wilt, swear by thy gracious self,

Which is the god of my idolatry,
And I'll believe thee.

Student 1 (*as Romeo*)   If my heart's dear love –

Student 2 (*as Juliet*)
Well, do not swear. Although I joy in thee,
I have no joy of this contract tonight:
It is too rash, too unadvis'd, too sudden,
Too like the lightning, which doth cease to be
Ere one can say 'It lightens.' Sweet, good night.
This bud of love, by summer's ripening breath,
May prove a beauteous flower when next we meet.
Good night, good night. As sweet repose and rest
Come to thy heart as that within my breast.

Student 1 (*as Romeo*)
O wilt thou leave me so unsatisfied?

Student 2 (*as Juliet*)
What satisfaction canst thou have tonight?

Student 1 (*as Romeo*)
Th'exchange of thy love's faithful vow for mine.

Student 2 (*as Juliet*)
I gave thee mine before thou didst request it,
And yet I would it were to give again.

Student 1 (*as Romeo*)
Wouldst thou withdraw it? For what purpose, love?

Student 2 (*as Juliet*)
But to be frank and give it thee again;
And yet I wish but for the thing I have.
My bounty is as boundless as the sea,
My love as deep: the more I give to thee
The more I have, for both are infinite.

Students 3 *and* **4** *awake. The moon and stars disappear. Lights are fully on.* **Students 1** *and* **2** *realise they have been caught.*

Student 2 (*as Juliet*)
  I hear some noise within. Dear love, adieu.

He quickly whispers in **Student 1***'s ear.* **Student 2** *grabs the script, opens it and reads.*

Act 2 Scene 3. Friar Laurence's cell.

  Stay but a little, I will come again.

He hands the script to **Student 3** *who takes on the role of the Friar.* **Student 3** *reads from the script as* **Students 2** *and* **4** *sit and listen.*

Student 3 (*as Friar*)
  I must upfill this osier cage of ours
  With baleful weeds and precious juiced flowers . . .

His voice trails off as the focus switches to **Student 1** *off to the side.*

Student 1 (*as Romeo*)
  O blessed blessed night I am afeard
  Being in night all this is but a dream
  Too flattering sweet to be substantial.

Student 2 *sneaks back to* **Student 1**.

Student 2 (*as Juliet*)
  Three words, dear Romeo, and goodnight indeed.
  If that thy bent of love be honourable,
  Thy purpose marriage, send me word tomorrow
  By one that I'll procure to come to thee,
  Where and what time thou wilt perform the rite,
  And all my fortunes at thy foot I'll lay,
  And follow thee my lord throughout the world.
  Tomorrow will I send.

Student 1 (*as Romeo*)   So strive my soul –

Student 2 (*as Juliet*)   A thousand times good night.

Student 2 *goes back to join the other two.*

Student 1 (*as Romeo*)
A thousand times the worse, to want thy light.
Love goes toward love as schoolboys from their books,
But love from love, toward school with heavy looks.

Student 1 *goes and sits down to listen with the others.*

Student 3 (*as Friar*)
Within the infant rind of this weak flower
Poison hath residence, and medicine power . . .

His voice trails off as the focus switches to **Students 1** *and* **2**
whispering to each other secretly.

Student 2 (*as Juliet*)   Romeo.

Student 1 (*as Romeo*)   My love.

Student 2 (*as Juliet*)   What o'clock tomorrow
Shall I send to thee?

Student 1 (*as Romeo*)   By the hour of nine.

Student 2 (*as Juliet*)   I will not fail. 'Tis twenty year till
then.

School bells.

Student 2   'Tis almost morning.

Knowing they have little time left, **Students 3** *and* **4** *quickly put the
flashlights away.* **Student 2** *runs and quickly kisses* **Student 1**.

Parting is such sweet sorrow
That I shall say good night till it be morrow.

Student 2 *shoves* **Student 1** *into the next scene.*

Act 2 Scene 3!

Student 1 (*as Romeo*)
Good morrow, father.

Student 3 (*as Friar*)
                      Benedicite.
What early tongue so sweet saluteth me?

Young son, it argues a distemper'd head
So soon to bid good morrow to thy bed.
Therefore thy earliness doth me assure
Thou are uprous'd with some distemperature;
Or, if not so, then here I hit it right:
Our Romeo hath not been in bed tonight.

Student 1 (*as Romeo*)
That last is true. The sweeter rest was mine.

Student 3 (*as Friar*)
God pardon sin! Wast thou with Rosaline?

Student 1 (*as Romeo*)
With Rosaline! My ghostly father, no.
I have forgot that name, and that name's woe.

Student 3 (*as Friar*)
That's my good son. But where hast thou been then?

Student 1 (*as Romeo*)
I'll tell thee ere thou ask it me again.
I have been feasting with mine enemy.

Student 3 (*as Friar*)
Be plain, good son, and homely in thy drift;
Riddling confession finds but riddling shrift.

Student 1 (*as Romeo*)
Then plainly know my heart's dear love is set
On the fair daughter of rich Capulet.
As mine on hers, so hers is set on mine,
And all combin'd save what thou must combine
By holy marriage. When, and where, and how
We met, we woo'd, and made exchange of vow
I'll tell thee as we pass; but this I pray,
That thou consent to marry us today.

Student 3 (*as Friar*)
Holy Saint Francis! What a change is here!
Is Rosaline, that thou didst love so dear,
So soon forsaken? Young men's love then lies

Not truly in their hearts but in their eyes.
Lo here upon thy cheek the stain doth sit
Of an old tear that is not wash'd off yet.
If ere thou wast thyself, and these woes thine,
Thou and these woes were all for Rosaline.
And art thou chang'd? Pronounce this sentence then:
Women may fall when there's no strength in men.

Student 1 (*as Romeo*)
Thou chid'st me oft for loving Rosaline.

Student 3 (*as Friar*)
For doting, not for loving, pupil mine.

Student 1 (*as Romeo*)
And bad'st me bury love.

Student 3 (*as Friar*)   Not in a grave
To lay one in, another out to have.

Student 1 (*as Romeo*)
I pray thee chide me not, her I love now
Doth grace for grace and love for love allow.
The other did not so.

Student 3 (*as Friar*)   O, she knew well
Thy love did read by rote that could not spell.

Ghostly voices are heard. The boys look about wildly.

Voices
A pair of star cross'd lovers bury their parents' strife.
A pair of star cross'd lovers bury their parents' strife.

The scene continues.

Student 3 (*as Friar*)
But come young waverer, come, go with me,
In one respect I'll thy assistant be.
For this alliance may so happy prove
To turn your households' rancour to pure love.

The bells ring again. **Students 2, 3,** *and* **4** *set up the classroom and sit at attention.* **Student 1** *tries to persuade them that they still have more time.*

Student 1   The clock struck nine.

The others do not move. **Student 1** *pushes them off their 'desks' and clears the playing area. He grabs the script, opens it, and hands it to* **Student 2**.

Student 1   The clock struck nine.

Student 2 *reads from the script.*

Student 2   The clock struck nine.

Student 1 *takes the script from* **Student 2** *and hands him the fabric.* **Student 2** *spreads it out like a bed sheet and waits for 'Romeo' as* **Students 1, 3** *and* **4** *tap out a steady clock-ticking rhythm.*

Student 3   Tick tock. Tick tock. Tick tock. Tick tock.

Students 1, 3 *and* **4** *start counting off the hours.*

Student 1   One.

Student 4   Two.

Student 3   Three.

Student 1   Four.

Student 4   Five.

Student 3   Six.

Student 1   Seven.

Student 4   Eight.

Student 3   Nine.

Student 1   Ten.

Student 4   Eleven.

Student 3   Twelve.

The three students make a drum riff and hit a final drum accent.

Student 2 (*as Juliet*)
The clock struck nine when I did send the Nurse,
In half an hour she promis'd to return.
Perchance she cannot meet him. That's not so.
O, she is lame.

He starts folding up the fabric.

Love's heralds should be thoughts
Which ten times faster glide than the sun's beams
Driving back shadows over lowering hills.
Therefore do nimble-pinion'd doves draw Love,
And therefore hath the wind-swift Cupid wings.
Now is the sun upon the highmost hill
Of this day's journey, and from nine till twelve
Is three long hours, yet she is not come.
Had she affections and warm youthful blood
She would be as swift in motion as a ball:

Student 2 *tosses the fabric into the air.* **Student 4** *catches it and takes on the role of the* **Nurse**.

My words would bandy her to my sweet love,
And his to me.
But old folks, many feign as they were dead –
Unwieldy, slow, heavy, and pale as lead.

Student 4 *enters the scene and moves the blocks together, forming a bed.*

O God she comes. O honey Nurse, what news?
Hast thou met with him?
Now good sweet Nurse, O Lord why look'st thou sad?
Though news be sad, yet tell them merrily,
If good, thou sham'st the music of sweet news
By playing it to me with so sour a face.

Student 4 (*as Nurse*)   I am aweary, give me leave awhile.
Fie, how my bones ache. What a jaunce have I had!

Student 2 (*as Juliet*)

I would thou hadst my bones and I thy news.
Nay come, I pray thee, speak: good, good Nurse, speak.

Student 4 (*as Nurse*)
Jesu, what haste. Can you not stay awhile?
Do you not see that I am out of breath?

Student 2 (*as Juliet*)
How art thou out of breath when thou hast breath
To say to me that thou art out of breath?
The excuse that thou dost make in this delay
Is longer than the tale thou dost excuse.
Is thy news good or bad? Answer to that,
Say either, and I'll stay the circumstance.

Student 2 *goes to* **Student 4** *imploringly*.

Let me be satisfied: is't good or bad?

Student 4 (*as Nurse*)   Well, you have made a simple
choice. You know not how to choose a man. Romeo? No,
not he. Though his face be better than any man's, yet his leg
excels all men's, and for a hand and a foot and a body,
though they be not to be talked on, yet they are past
compare. He is not the flower of courtesy, but I'll warrant
him as gentle as a lamb. Go thy ways, wench, serve God.

He lies down on the 'bed.' **Student 2** *goes to* **Student 4** *for more
information*.

What?

Student 2 (*as Juliet*)
No, no. But all this did I know before.
What says he of our marriage? What of that?

Student 4 (*as Nurse*)
Lord, how my head aches! What a head have I:
It beats as it would fall in twenty pieces.

Student 2 *begins massaging* **Student 4**'s *temples*.

My back o' t'other side—ah, my back, my back!

Student 2 *begins massaging* **Student 4**'s *back.*

> Beshrew your heart for sending me about
> To catch my death with jauncing up and down.

Student 2 (*as Juliet*)

> I'faith I am sorry that thou art not well.
> Sweet, sweet, sweet Nurse, tell me, what says my love?

Student 4 (*as Nurse*)

> Your love says like an honest gentleman,
> And a courteous, and a kind, and a handsome,
> And I warrant a virtuous – Where is your mother?

Student 4 *begins listening for any sound outside the room.*

Student 2 (*as Juliet*)

> Where is my mother? Why, she is within.
> Where should she be? How oddly thou repliest.
> 'Your love says, like an honest gentleman,
> Where is your mother?'

Student 4 (*as Nurse*)

> 　　　　　　　　O God's lady dear,
> Are you so hot? Marry, come up, I trow.
> Is this the poultice for my aching bones?
> Henceforward do your messages yourself.

Student 4 *starts to exit.* **Student 2** *stops him.*

Student 2 (*as Juliet*)

> Here's such a coil. Come, what says Romeo?

Student 4 (*as Nurse*)

> Have you got leave to go to shrift today?

Student 2 (*as Juliet*)   I have.

Student 4 (*as Nurse*)

> Then hie you hence to Friar Laurence' cell.
> There stays a husband to make you a wife.

They embrace.

Student 2 (*as Juliet*)
  Hie to high fortune! Honest Nurse, farewell.

Student 4 *grabs the copy of* Romeo and Juliet *and reads from it.
The rest of the* **Students** *set up the next scene.*

Student 4   Act Two Scene Six.

Student 3 *takes the book and reads from it.*

Student 3   Friar Laurence' cell.

Student 1   Romeo waits.

Student 2   Juliet enters.

Students 1 *and* **2** *kneel facing each other.*

Students 1 and 2   The wedding.

Student 1 *grabs the book from* **Student 3** *and reads.*

Student 1 (*as Romeo*)   Ah, Juliet, if the measure of thy joy
  Be heap'd like mine –

Student 4 *snatches the book from* **Student 1**. **Student 1** *takes
it back and returns to kneeling with* **Student 2**.

Student 1 (*as Romeo*)   Ah, Juliet, if the measure of thy joy
  Be heap'd like mine

Student 3 *snatches the book from* **Student 1**. **Student 2** *takes
it back and returns to kneeling with* **Student 1**.

Student 2 (*as Juliet*)
  But my true love is grown to such excess –

Student 4 *snatches the book from* **Student 2**. *A chase ensues with*
Students 3 *and* **4** *tossing the script back and forth to keep it from*
Students 1 *and* **2**. *Finally,* **Student 2** *is pushed to the ground
and* **Student 1** *is held back by* **Student 4**, *while* **Student 3**
rips a page from the script. He holds the page up and reads from it.

Student 3
  'But my true love is grown to such excess –'

He tears the page to pieces. **Students 1** *and* **2** *are at a loss as to what to do. They search their minds for some text. Then some words come to* **Student 1**.

Student 1   Shall I compare thee to a summer's day?!

Ecstatic that they have found their own vows, **Students 1** *and* **2** *kneel and work through the sonnet together.*

Student 1   Thou art more lovely and – and –

Student 2   – and more temperate!
    Rough winds do shake the darling buds of May,

Student 1 and 2   And summer's lease hath all too short a date.

Students 3 *and* **4** *start to taunt* **Students 1** *and* **2** *with the 'Love Theme' from Zefirelli's Romeo and Juliet and circle them.*

Student 1   Sometime too hot the eye of heaven shines,

Student 2   And often is –

Students 1 and 2   – his gold complexion dimm'd;

Student 1   And every fair from fair sometime declines,
    By chance, or – or –

Student 2   – or nature's changing course untrimmed
    But thy eternal summer shall not fade

Student 1   Nor lose possession of that fair thou ow'st, –

Student 2
    Nor shall Death brag thou wand'rest in his shade
    When in eternal lines to time thou grow'st.

Students 3 *and* **4** *try to pull* **Students 1** *and* **2** *apart.*

Student 1 and 2
    So long as men can breathe or eyes can see,
    So long lives this, and this gives life to thee.!

Students 3 *and* **4** *succeed in pulling them apart and* **Student 3** *hits* **Student 1** *across the face with the book. They all stop* *paralyzed by the sudden violence.* **Student 3**, *shocked at what he is done, throws the book down. After a pause, he goes to* **Student 1**.

Student 3   Let me not to the marriage of true minds
   Admit impediments; love is not love
   Which alters when it alteration finds
   Or bends with the remover to remove

Student 3 and 2   O, no –

Student 2 *goes to* **Student 3** *and takes his hand.*

Student 2   – it is an ever-fixèd mark
   That looks on tempests and is never shaken;

Students 3 and 2   It is the star to every wand'ring bark –
   Whose worth's unknown, although his height be taken.

Student 4 *goes and joins hands with the others.*

Students 3, 2 and 4
   Love's not Time's fool, though rosy lips and cheeks
   Within his bending sickle's compass come;

Student 1 *joins hands with the rest.*

Student 3, 2, 4 and 1
   Love alters not with his brief hours and weeks,
   But bears it out even to the edge of doom.

Students 1 *and* **2** *join hands, kneeling facing each other.* **Student 3** *stands in front of them, officiating the ceremony.* **Student 4** *looks on as a witness.*

Student 1   If this be error, and upon me proved,
   I never writ, nor no man ever loved.

Student 1 *and* **Student 2** *kiss.*

Student 3   So smile the heavens upon this holy act
   That after-hours with sorrow chide us not.

School bells ring. **Students 2**, **3** *and* **4** *start to set up their school room again.* **Student 1** *stops them. He takes his sweater off as if he is tearing off a layer of skin that has been stifling him.*

Student 1   Amos, amas, amamus, amatis, amant!

He throws the sweater on the ground. **Student 2** *takes his sweater off in the same fashion and tosses it in a pile with the other sweater.*

Student 2   The business of a man is to govern the world and the destiny of a woman is to charm and influence it!

Students 3 *and* **4** *tear their sweaters off and add them to the pile.*

Student 3   Without women men soon resume the savage state!

Student 4   Let us particularly note the difference in character between the two sexes, a difference so great that one might suppose them members of two different races!

Student 2 *grabs the composition books and adds them to the pile of sweaters.*

Student 2   Thou shalt not lie, steal, kill, cheat –

All the **Students** *take off their ties and add them to the pile.*

All   LUST!!

Student 1 *takes the pile of sweaters and books and puts them in the hiding space under the floorboards. The boys are bursting, ravenous, desperate to go on with the tale and their adventure. Thunder rolls and whispered voices swirl around the boys. The ghostly voices alternately frighten and excite the boys sending them to the edge.*

Student 1 (*V.O.*)
  Two households both alike in dignity
  In fair Verona where we lay our scene . . .

Student 2 (*V.O.*)
  Romeo, Romeo, wherefore art thou Romeo . . .

Student 3 (*V.O.*)
  Oh then I see, Queen Mab hath been with you . . .

Student 4 (*V.O.*)
  There stays a husband to make you a wife . . .

All *(V.O.)* *(overlapping each other)* A pair of star-cross'd lovers take their life . . .

Student 1 *(V.O.)*
The fearful passage of their death-mark'd love
Is now the two hours' traffic of our stage.

All   *(overlapping and repeating and building to a crescendo)*
The fearful passage of their death-mark'd love
Is now the two hours' traffic of our stage!

A huge clap of thunder and the boys hurl themselves into the next scene.

Student 2 *(as Benvolio) is following* **Student 3** *(as Mercutio) who is agitated, anxious.*

Student 2 *(as Benvolio)*
I pray thee, good Mercutio, let's retire;
The day is hot, the Capulets abroad,
And if we meet we shall not 'scape a brawl,
For now these hot days is the mad blood stirring.

Student 2 *(as Mercutio)*   Thou art like one of these fellows that, when he enters the confines of tavern, claps me his sword upon the table and says 'God send me no need of thee!' and by the operation of the second cup draws him on the drawer, when indeed there is no need.

Student 2 *(as Benvolio)*   Am I like such a fellow?

Student 3 *(as Mercutio)*   Come, come, thou art as hot a Jack in thy mood as any in Italy. Thou hast quarrelled with a man for coughing in the street, because he hath wakened thy dog that hath lain asleep in the sun. Didst thou not fall out with a tailor for wearing his new doublet before Easter; with another for tying his new shoes with old riband? And yet thou wilt tutor me from quarrelling!

Student 4 *jumps in as* **Tybalt**.

Student 2 *(as Benvolio)*   By my head, here come the Capulets.

Student 3 *(as Mercutio)*   By my heel, I care not.

Student 4 (*as Tybalt*)   Gentlemen, good e'en: a word with one of you.

Student 3 (*as Mercutio*)   And but one word with one of us? Couple it with something, make it a word and a blow.

Student 4 (*as Tybalt*)   You shall find me apt enough to that, sir, and you will give me occasion.

Student 3 (*as Mercutio*)   Could you not take some occasion without giving?

Student 4 (*as Tybalt*)   Mercutio, thou . . . consortest with Romeo.

Student 3 (*as Mercutio*)   Consort? What, dost thou make us minstrels? And thou make minstrels of us, look to hear nothing but discords.

Student 3 *grabs the fabric.*

Student 2 (*as Benvolio*)
We talk here in the public haunt of men.
Either withdraw unto some private place,
And reason coldly of your grievances,
Or else depart. Here all eyes gaze on us.

Student 3 (*as Mercutio*)
Men's eyes were made to look, and let them gaze.
I will not budge for no man's pleasure, I.

Student 3 *hands one end of the fabric to* **Student 4**, *challenging him to a fight.*

Here's my fiddlestick, here's that shall make you dance. Zounds, consort!

Student 1 *jumps in as* **Romeo**.

Student 4 (*as Tybalt*)
Well, peace be with you, sir, here comes my man.

The fabric is held taut between the two of them as they circle each other.

Student 3 (*as Mercutio*)

But I'll be hang'd, sir, if he wear your livery.
Marry, go before to field, he'll be your follower.
Your worship in that sense may call him 'man'.

Student 4 (*as Tybalt*)
Romeo, the love I bear thee can afford
No better term than this: thou art a villain!

Student 1 (*as Romeo*)
Tybalt, the reason that I have to love thee
Doth much excuse the appertaining rage
To such a greeting: villain am I none,
Therefore farewell. I see thou know'st me not.

Student 1 *starts to exit.*

Student 4 (*as Tybalt*)
Boy, this shall not excuse the injuries
That thou hast done me, therefore turn and draw!

Student 1 *grabs one end of the fabric from* **Student 3** *and climbs up the fabric toward* **Student 4**.

Student 1 (*as Romeo*)   I do protest I never injured thee,
But love thee better than thou canst devise
Till thou shalt know the reason of my love.
And so, good Capulet, which name I tender
As dearly as mine own, be satisfied.

Student 1 *kneels in front of* **Student 4**. *Appalled,* **Student 3** *grabs the fabric from* **Student 1**.

Student 3 (*as Mercutio*)
O calm, dishonourable, vile submission:
Alla stoccata carries it away!
Tybalt, you rat-catcher, will you walk?

Student 3 *and* **Student 4** *circle each other.*

Student 4 (*as Tybalt*)   What wouldst thou have with me?

Student 3 (*as Mercutio*)   Good King of Cats, nothing but one of your nine lives. That I mean to make bold withal, and, as you shall use me hereafter, dry-beat the rest of the eight. Will you pluck your sword out of his pitcher by the ears? Make haste, lest mine be about your ears ere it be out.

Student 4 (*as Tybalt*)   I am for you.

Student 1 (*as Romeo*)   Gentle Mercutio, put thy rapier up.

Student 3 (*as Mercutio*)   Come sir, your passado.

They fight; it is fierce, violent, and dangerous. **Student 1** *tries to stop the fight, but* **Student 2** *holds him back.*

Student 1 (*as Romeo*)
Draw, Benvolio, beat down their weapons.
Gentlemen, for shame, forbear this outrage.
Tybalt, Mercutio! The Prince expressly hath
Forbid this bandying in Verona streets.
Hold, Tybalt! Good Mercutio!

Student 1 *finally breaks away from* **Student 2** *and grabs the fabric. As a result,* **Student 3** *withstands a fatal blow.*

Student 3 (*as Mercutio*)   I am hurt.
A plague on both your houses. I am sped.

Student 2 (*as Benvolio*)   What, art thou hurt?

Student 3 (*as Mercutio*)
Ay, ay, a scratch, a scratch. Marry, 'tis enough.
Go, fetch a surgeon.

Student 1 (*as Romeo*)   Courage, man, the hurt cannot be much.

Student 3 (*as Mercutio*)   No, 'tis not so deep as a well, nor so wide as a church door, but 'tis enough, 'twill serve. Ask for me tomorrow and you shall find me a grave man. I am peppered, I warrant, for this world. A plague on both your houses! Zounds, a dog, a rat, a mouse, a cat, to scratch a man to death.

Student 3 *lunges for* **Student 4**.

A braggart, a rogue, a villain that fights by the book of arithmetic.

Student 1 *holds* **Student 3** *back.* **Student 3** *holds on to*
Student 1, *barely able to stand up.*

Why the devil came you between us? I was hurt under your
arm.

Student 1 (*as Romeo*)   I thought all for the best.

Student 3 *backs away from* **Student 1** *leaving one end of the*
fabric with him. As the distance grows between them, the fabric spreads
out like a river of blood.

Student 3 (*as Mercutio*)   A plague on both your houses,
    They have made worms' meat of me. I have it,
    And soundly too. A plague on both your houses!

Student 3 *leaves* **Student 1** *holding the fabric.*

Student 1 (*as Romeo*)
    This day's black fate on mo days doth depend:
    This but begins the woe others must end.
    Away to heaven respective lenity,
    And fire-ey'd fury be my conduct now!

Student 1 *stands and confronts* **Student 4**.
    Now, Tybalt, take the villain back again
    That late thou gav'st me, for Mercutio's soul
    Is but a little way above our heads,
    Staying for thine to keep him company!
    Either thou, or I, or both must go with him!

Student 1 *presents one end of the fabric to* **Student 4**, *challenging*
him to a fight.

Student 4 (*as Tybalt*)
    Thou wretched boy, that didst consort him here,
    Shalt with him hence!

He grabs one end of the fabric.

Student 1 (*as Romeo*)   This shall determine that!

Student 1 *runs to* **Student 4** *and strangles him to death with the fabric.* **Student 1** *remains paralysed kneeling over* **Student 4***'s body.* **Student 2** *tries to rouse* **Student 1** *who cannot move.*

Student 2 (*as Benvolio*)   Romeo, away, be gone,
  The citizens are up, and Tybalt slain!
  Stand not amaz'd. The Prince will doom thee death
  If thou art taken. Hence, be gone, away!

Student 1 (*as Romeo*)   O, I am fortune's fool.

Student 2 *grabs* **Student 1** *and pushes him off.*

Student 2 (*as Benvolio*)   Why dost thou stay?!

All the **Students** *form a clump as the* **Prince***.*

All (*in a round*)   Where are the vile beginners of this fray?

Student 2 (*as* **Benvolio**) *breaks out of the formation and kneels facing the front.*

Student 2 (*as Benvolio*)   O noble Prince, I can discover all
  The unlucky manage of this fatal brawl.
  There lies the man, slain by young Romeo,
  That slew thy kinsman, brave Mercutio.

Student 3 (*as* **Lady Capulet**) *breaks out of the formation and kneels facing the front.*

Student 3 (*as Lady Capulet*)
  Tybalt, my cousin, O my brother's child!
  Prince, as thou art true,
  For blood of ours shed blood of Montague!

Students 1 and 4   Benvolio, who began this bloody fray?

Student 3 (*as Lady Capulet*)
  He is a kinsman to the Montague!
  Affection makes him false. He'll speak not true!
  I beg for justice, which thou, Prince, must give.
  Romeo slew Tybalt. Romeo must not live!

Student 1   Romeo slew him.

Student 4   He slew Mercutio.

Students 1 and 4   Who now the price of his dear blood
doth owe?

Student 2 (*as Benvolio*)
   Not Romeo, Prince, he was Mercutio's friend;
   His fault concludes but what the law should end,
   The life of Tybalt.

Student 1   And for that offence
   Immediately we do exile him hence.

As each of the **Students** *joins in with text, they join the* **Prince***'s
formation.*

+Student 4   I have an interest in your heart's proceeding;
   My blood for your rude brawls doth lie a-bleeding.

+Student 2   But I'll amerce you with so strong a fine
   That you shall all repent the loss of mine.

+Student 3   I will be deaf to pleading and excuses;
   Nor tears nor prayers shall purchase out abuses.
   Therefore use none. Let Romeo hence in haste,

All (*spoken in a round*) Else, when he is found, that hour is his
last!!

Act Two

All (*V.O.*) Let Romeo hence in haste,

(*in a round*) Else, when he is found, that hour is his last!

Student 2 *furiously pushes* **Student 1** *off, urging him to escape.*

Student 2 Why dost thou stay!

They all run off after **Student 1**, *calling and searching frantically for him through the streets of Verona.*

All Romeo!

Student 2 *suddenly becomes* **Juliet**.

Student 2 (*as Juliet*) Gallop apace, you fiery-footed steeds,
  Toward Phoebus' lodging. Such a wagoner
  As Phaethon would whip you to the west
  And bring in cloudy night immediately.

Student 2 *takes the fabric and spreads it out on the floor. It becomes a bed which he prepares for the wedding night.*

  Spread thy close curtain, love-performing night,
  That runaway's eyes may wink, and Romeo
  Leap to these arms untalk'd-of and unseen.
  Lovers can see to do their amorous rites
  By their own beauties; or, if love be blind,
  It best agrees with night. Come, civil night,
  Thou sober-suited matron, all in black.
  And learn me how to lose a winning match
  Play'd for a pair of stainless maidenhoods.
  Hood my unmann'd blood, bating in my cheeks,
  With thy black mantle, till strange love, grow bold,
  Think true love acted simple modesty.
  Come night, come Romeo, come thou day in night,
  For thou wilt lie upon the wings of night
  Whiter than new snow upon a raven's back.
  Come gentle night, come loving black-brow'd night,
  Give me my Romeo; and when I shall die

Take him and cut him out in little stars,
And he will make the face of heaven so fine
That all the world will be in love with night,
And pay no worship to the garish sun.

Student 4 *runs back on frantic out of breath. He grabs the script and frantically flips through it, desperate to find out what happens next.*

O, I have bought the mansion of a love
But not possess'd it, and though I am sold,
Not yet enjoy'd. So tedious is this day
As is the night before some festival
To an impatient child that hath new robes
And may not wear them.

Student 1 *sees* **Student 4**.

                              O, here comes my Nurse.
And she brings news, and every tongue that speaks
But Romeo's name speaks heavenly eloquence.

Student 1 *grabs at* **Student 4**, *desperate for some news.*

Now, Nurse, what news? Why dost thou wring thy hands?

Student 4 (*as Nurse*)   Ah welladay, he's dead. (*He finally looks up from the script.*) He's dead. He's dead!

He throws the script down.

We are undone, lady, we are undone.
Alack the day, he's gone, he's killed, he's dead.

Student 2 (*as Juliet*)   Can heaven be so envious?

Student 4 (*as Nurse*)   Romeo can,
Though heaven cannot. O Romeo . . . Romeo . . . .
Who ever would have thought it? Romeo!

Student 2 (*as Juliet*)
What devil art thou that dost torment me thus?
This torture should be roar'd in dismal hell.
Hath Romeo slain himself?

He runs to grab the script and starts flipping through it.

If he be slain say 'Ay', or if not, 'No'.
Brief sounds determine of my weal or woe.

Student 4 *grabs the script away.*

Student 4 (*as Nurse*)
I saw the wound, I saw it with mine eyes
– God save the mark – here on his manly breast.
A piteous corse, a bloody piteous corse,
Pale, pale as ashes, all bedaub'd in blood,
All in gore-blood. I swounded at the sight.

Student 2 *breaks away.*

Student 2 (*as Juliet*)
O break, my heart. Poor bankrupt, break at once.

Student 4 (*as Nurse*)
O Tybalt, Tybalt, the best friend I had.
O courteous Tybalt, honest gentleman.
That ever I should live to see thee dead.

Student 2 (*as Juliet*)
What storm is this that blows so contrary?
Is Romeo slaughter'd and is Tybalt dead?
My dearest cousin and my dearer lord?

Student 4 (*as Nurse*)
Tybalt is gone and Romeo banished.
Romeo that kill'd him, he is banished!

Student 2 (*as Juliet*)
O God! Did Romeo's hand shed Tybalt's blood?

Student 4 (*as Nurse*)   It did, it did, alas the day, it did!

Student 2 (*as Juliet*)
O, that deceit should dwell in such a gorgeous palace.

They are left speechless.

Student 4 (*as Nurse*)
These griefs, these woes, these sorrows make me old.
Shame come to Romeo.

Student 2 *grabs* **Student 4** *violently.*

Student 2 (*as Juliet*)   Blister'd be thy tongue
For such a wish! He was not born to shame.
Upon his brow shame is asham'd to sit.

Student 4 (*as Nurse*)
Will you speak well of him that kill'd your cousin?

Student 2 (*as Juliet*)
Shall I speak ill of him that is my husband?!

Student 2 *throws* **Student 4** *to the ground.*

Some word there was, worser than Tybalt's death,
That murder'd me. I would forget it fain,
But O, it presses to my memory
Like damned guilty deeds to sinners' minds.
'Tybalt is dead and Romeo-banished.'
That 'banished', that one word 'banished',
Hath slain ten thousand Tybalts: Tybalt's death
Was woe enough, if it had ended there.
Or if sour woe delights in fellowship
And needly will be rank'd with other griefs,
Why follow'd not, when she said 'Tybalt's dead',
Thy father or thy mother, nay or both,
Which modern lamentations might have mov'd?
But with a rearward following Tybalt's death,
'Romeo is banished': to speak that word
Is father, mother, Tybalt, Romeo, Juliet,
All slain, all dead. 'Romeo is banished',
There is no end, no limit, measure, bound,
In that word's death. No words can that woe sound.

Student 4 *goes to* **Student 2** *to comfort him.*

Student 4 (*as Nurse*)   Hie to your chamber. I'll find Romeo
To comfort you. I wot well where he is.
Hark ye, your Romeo will be here at night.
I'll to him. He is hid at Laurence' cell.

Student 2 *gives his school ring to* **Student 4**.

Student 2 (*as Juliet*)
O find him, give this ring to my true knight
And bid him come to take his last farewell.

Student 4 *goes looking for 'Romeo'.* **Student 3** *enters, looking for*
Student 1.

Student 3 (*as Friar*)   Romeo . . . Romeo . . .
Romeo, come forth, come forth, thou fearful man.

Student 1 *enters.*

Student 1 (*as Romeo*)
Father, what news? What is the Prince's doom?
What sorrow craves acquaintance at my hand
That I yet know not?

Student 3 (*as Friar*)   Too familiar
Is my dear son with such sour company.
I bring thee tidings of the Prince's doom.

Student 1 (*as Romeo*)
What less than doomsday is the Prince's doom?

Student 3 (*as Friar*)
A gentler judgement vanish'd from his lips:
Not body's death but body's banishment.

Student 1 (*as Romeo*)
Ha, banishment? Be merciful, say 'death'.
For exile hath more terror in his look,
Much more than death. Do not say 'banishment'.

Student 1 *starts to leave.* **Student 3** *stops him.*

Student 3 (*as Friar*)
Hence from Verona art thou banished.
Be patient, for the world is broad and wide.

Student 1 (*as Romeo*)
There is no world without Verona's walls.

Student 1 *goes to leave again, and again* **Student 3** *stops him.*

Student 3 (*as Friar*)
    This is dear mercy and thou seest it not.

Student 1 (*as Romeo*)
    'Tis torture and not mercy. Heaven is here
    Where Juliet lives –

Student 1 *goes to leave again. This time* **Student 3** *grabs him and holds him.*

Student 3 (*as Friar*)   Thou fond mad man, hear me a little speak.

Student 1 (*as Romeo*)   O, thou wilt speak again of banishment.

Student 3 (*as Friar*)
    I'll give thee armour to keep off that word,
    Adversity's sweet milk, philosophy,
    To comfort thee though thou art banished.

Student 1 *breaks away.*

Student 1 (*as Romeo*)
    Yet 'banished'? Hang up philosophy.
    Unless philosophy can make a Juliet,
    Displant a town, reverse a Prince's doom,
    It helps not, it prevails not. Talk no more.

Student 1 *again goes to leave and is held back by* **Student 3**.

Student 3 (*as Friar*)   O, then I see that mad men have no ears.

Student 1 (*as Romeo*)
    How should they when that wise men have no eyes?

Student 3 *grabs* **Student 1** *and tries to sit him down.*

Student 3 (*as Friar*)   Let me dispute with thee of thy estate!

Student 1 *breaks away.*

Student 1 (*as Romeo*)
    Thou canst not speak of that thou dost not feel.

Wert thou as young as I, Juliet thy love,
An hour but married, Tybalt murdered,
Doting like me, and like me banished,
Then mightst thou speak, then mightst thou tear thy hair
And fall upon the ground as I do now,
Taking the measure of an unmade grave.

Knocking. **Students 3** *and* **2** *look around panicked. Have they been caught?*

Student 3 (*as Friar*)   Arise, one knocks. Good Romeo, hide thyself.

Student 1 (*as Romeo*)
Not I, unless the breath of heartsick groans
Mist-like enfold me from the search of eyes.

Three more knocks. **Students 1** *and* **3** *run around, trying to tidy up the room and hide all evidence of their goings-on.*

Student 3   Hark how they knock.

Student 2   – Who's there?

Student 3   – Romeo, arise, Thou wilt be taken.

More knocks.

Student 2   – Stay awhile.

Student 3
Stand up. Run to my study. (*More knocks.*) By and by.
God's will,
What simpleness is this? I come, I come.
Who knocks so hard? Whence come you, what's your will?

Student 4 (*as Nurse*)
Let me come in and you shall know my errand.
I come from Lady Juliet.

Relief all around.

Student 3 (*as Friar*)   Welcome then.

Student 4 *enters.*

Student 4 (*as Nurse*)   O holy Friar, O, tell me, holy Friar,
Where is my lady's lord, where's Romeo?

Student 1 *approaches* **Student 4**.

Student 1 (*as Romeo*)
Spak's thou of Juliet? How is it with her?
Doth not she think me an old murderer
Now I have stain'd the childhood of our joy
With blood remov'd but little from her own?
Where is she? And how doth she? And what says
My conceal'd lady to our cancell'd love?

Student 4 (*as Nurse*)
O, she says nothing, sir, but weeps and weeps,
And now falls on her bed, and then starts up,
And Tybalt calls, and then on Romeo cries,
And then down falls again.

Student 1 (*as Romeo*)   As if that name,
Shot from the deadly level of a gun,
Did murder her, as that name's cursed hand
Murder'd her kinsman. O, tell me, Friar, tell me,
In what vile part of this anatomy
Doth my name lodge? Tell me that I may sack
The hateful mansion.

He grabs the fabric and goes to hang himself.

Student 3 (*as Friar*)   Hold thy desperate hand!
Art thou a man? Thy form cries out thou art.
Thy tears are womanish, thy wild acts denote
The unreasonable fury of a beast.
Unseemly woman in a seeming man,
And ill-beseeming beast in seeming both!
Thou hast amaz'd me. By my holy order,
I thought thy disposition better temper'd.
Hast thou slain Tybalt? Wilt thou slay thyself?
And slay thy lady that in thy life lives,
By doing damned hate upon thyself?
What, rouse thee, man. Thy Juliet is alive,

For whose dear sake thou wast but lately dead.
There art thou happy. Tybalt would kill thee,
But thou slew'st Tybalt. There art thou happy.
The law that threaten'd death becomes thy friend
And turns it to exile. There art thou happy.
A pack of blessings light upon thy back;
Happiness courts thee in her best array;
But like a mishav'd and a sullen wench
Thou pout'st upon thy fortune and thy love.
Take heed, take heed, for such die miserable.

Go before, Nurse. Commend me to thy lady
And bid her hasten all the house to bed,
Which heavy sorrow makes them apt unto.
Romeo is coming.

Student 4 (*as Nurse*)
Oh Lord I could have stayed here all the night
To hear good counsel. Oh what learning is.
My lord, I'll tell my lady you will come.

Student 4 *hands* **Student 2**'s *class ring to* **Student 1**.

Student 4 (*as Nurse*)   Here sir, a ring she bid me give you, sir.

Student 1 (*as Romeo*)   How well my comfort is reviv'd by this.

Student 3 (*as Friar*)
Go hence, good night, and here stands all your state:
Either be gone before the Watch be set,
Or by the break of day disguis'd from hence,
Sojourn in Mantua. I'll find out your man,
And he shall signify from time to time
Every good hap to you that chances here.
Go, get thee to thy love as was decreed,
Ascend her chamber, hence, and comfort her.

Music is magically heard. **Students 1**, **2** *and* **3** *clear the space of furniture.* **Student 4** *grabs a tray full of candles.* **Students 3** *and* **4** *each light a candle.* **Students 1** *and* **2** *light a long match off of*

each of those candles and light a third candle together. **Students 3**
and **4** *light dozens of other candles as* **Students 1** *and* **2** *set them
all over the room, filling it with blazing points of light. When all the
candles are lit* **Students 1** *and* **2** *stand in the middle of the sea of
candles. They kiss.* **Students 3** *and* **4** *turn away to give them
privacy.*

Students 3 and 4
    These blue-veined violets whereupon we lean
    Never can blab, nor know what we mean.

Students 1 *and* **2** *take each other to the floor and fall asleep in each
other's arms.*

Later. Bells ring. **Student 1** *wakes up and gently gives* **Student 2**
a kiss goodbye and starts to leave. **Student 2** *grabs him.*

Student 2 *(as Juliet)*   Wilt thou be gone? It is not yet near day.
    It was the nightingale and not the lark
    That pierc'd the fearful hollow of thine ear.
    Nightly she sings on yon pomegranate tree.
    Believe me, love, it was the nightingale.

Student 1 *(as Romeo)*
    It was the lark, the herald of the morn,
    No nightingale. Look, love, what envious streaks
    Do lace the severing clouds in yonder east.
    Night's candles are burnt out, and jocund day
    Stands tiptoe on the misty mountain tops.
    I must be gone and live, or stay and die.

Student 1 *again goes to leave and is stopped by* **Student 2**.

Student 2 *(as Juliet)*   Yond light is not daylight, I know
it, I.
    It is some meteor that the sun exhales
    To be to thee this night a torch-bearer
    And light thee on thy way to Mantua.
    Therefore stay yet: thou need'st not to be gone.

They kiss passionately. **Student 2** *takes* **Student 1** *down to the
floor.*

Student 1 (*as Romeo*)
Let me be ta'en, let me be put to death,
I am content, so thou wilt have it so.
I'll say yon grey is not the morning's eye,
'Tis but the pale reflex of Cynthia's brow.
Nor that is not the lark whose notes do beat
The vaulty heaven so high above our heads.
I have more care to stay than will to go.
Come death, and welcome. Juliet wills it so.

Student 4 *enters and starts clearing up the candles.*

Student 4 (*as Nurse*)   Madam.

Student 2 (*as Juliet*)   Nurse?

Student 4 (*as Nurse*)
Your lady mother is coming to your chamber.
The day is broke, be wary, look about.

Student 4 *hands over the script to* **Student 3**.

Student 2 (*as Juliet*)
Then, window, let day in and let life out.

Student 1 (*as Romeo*)
Farewell, farewell, one kiss and I'll descend.

Student 2 (*as Juliet*)
Art thou gone so? Love, lord, ay husband, friend,
I must hear from thee every day in the hour,
For in a minute there are many days.

Student 1 (*as Romeo*)   Farewell.
I will omit no opportunity.
That may convey my greetings, love, to thee.

Student 2 (*as Juliet*)
O think'st thou we shall ever meet again?

Student 1 (*as Romeo*)
I doubt it not, and all these woes shall serve
For sweet discourses in our times to come.

After a quick kiss, **Student 1** *exits.* **Student 2** *begins to help* **Students 3** *and* **4** *clear the candles.*

Student 2 (*as Juliet*)
O Fortune, Fortune! All men call thee fickle;
If thou art fickle, what dost thou with him
That is renown'd for faith? Be fickle, Fortune,
For then I hope thou wilt not keep him long,
But send him back.

Student 2 *sits at attention as* **Student 3** *enters the scene, reading from the script.*

Student 2 (*as Juliet*)   Who is't that calls?

Student 3 (*as Lady Capulet*)   Why, how now Juliet?

Student 2 (*as Juliet*)   Madam, I am not well.

Student 3 (*as Lady Capulet*)
I come to tell thee joyful tidings, girl.

Relieved, **Student 2** *laughs and runs and hugs* **Student 3** *from behind, reading over his shoulder.*

Student 2 (*as Juliet*)
And joy comes well in such a needy time.
What are they, I beseech your ladyship?

Student 2 *wrestles with him joyfully. They laugh as* **Student 3** *tries to read from the script in the midst of all the horseplay.*

Student 3 (*as Lady Capulet*)
Well, well, thou hast a careful father, child;
One who, to put thee from thy heaviness,
Hath sorted out a sudden day of joy,
That thou expect'st not, nor I look'd not for.

Student 2 *tickles him.*

Student 2 (*as Juliet*)
Madam, in happy time. What day is that?

Student 3 (*as Lady Capulet*)
Marry, my child, early next Thursday morn

The gallant, young, and noble gentleman,
The County Paris, at Saint Peter's Church,
Shall happily make thee there a joyful bride!

The horseplay suddenly stops.

Student 2 (*as Juliet*)
Now by Saint Peter's Church, and Peter too,
He shall not make me there a joyful bride.
I wonder at this haste, that I must wed
Ere he that should be husband comes to woo.

Student 2 *runs to* **Student 3**, *falls to his knees and clutches at him.*

I pray you tell my lord and father, madam,
I will not marry yet. And when I do, I swear
It shall be Romeo, whom you know I hate,
Rather than Paris!

Students 1 *and* **4** *start marching.*

Student 3 (*as Lady Capulet*)
Here comes your father, tell him so yourself,
And see how he will take it at your hands.

Student 1, **Student 4** *and* **Student 3** *join together and form a clump as* **Lord Capulet** *and push* **Student 2** *to the ground.*

Student 3   Hang thee young baggage!

Student 4   Disobedient wretch!

Student 1   I tell thee what:

Students 3, 1 and 4 (*spoken in a round*)   Get thee to church a Thursday!

Student 3   Or never after look me in the face. Speak not!

Student 4   Reply not!

Student 1   Do not answer me!

Students 1, 3 and 4   My fingers itch! God's bread, it makes me mad!

Student 3   Day!

Student 4   Night!

Student 1   Work!

Student 3   Play!

Student 4   Alone!

Student 1   In company!

Students 1, 3 and 4   Still my care hath been to have her match'd! And having now provided a gentleman –

Student 3   Of noble parentage!

Student 4   Of fair demesnes!

Student 1   Youthful and nobly lign'd!

Student 3   Stuffed, as they say, with honourable parts!

Student 4   Proportion'd as one's thought would wish a man –

Students 1, 3 and 4   And then to have –

Student 3 *moves out of the clump towards* **Student 2**,

Student 3   A wretched puling fool!
A whining mammet!
In her fortune's tender, to answer:

The other two get caught up in **Student 3**'s *energy and they taunt* **Student 2**, *laughing.*

Student 3   'I'll not wed'.

Student 4   'I cannot love'.

Student 1   'I am too young, I pray you pardon me'!

Student 1 *wraps the fabric around* **Student 2** *trapping him as the others undo his trousers and pull his trousers down leaving him in his boxers.*

Students 1, 3 and 4   But, as you will not wed, I'll pardon you!

Student 3   Graze where you will!

Student 4   You shall not house with me!

They push him centre stage and laugh at him with his pants down.

Student 1   Look to't!

Student 3   Think on't!

Student 4   I do not use to jest.

Students 1, 3 and 4   Thursday is near.

Student 1 *grabs* **Student 2** *from behind.*

Student 3   Lay hand on heart!

Student 4   Advise!

Student 1   And you be mine, I'll give you to my friend!

Students 1, 3 and 4   And you be not –

Students 3 *and* **4** *begin punching* **Student 2**. **Student 1** *backs away horrified.*

Student 3   Hang!

Student 4   Beg!

Student 3 and 4   Starve!

Student 3   Die in the streets!

Students 3 *and* **4** *throw* **Student 2** *to the ground and kick him.*

Students 3 and 4
    For by my soul I'll ne'er acknowledge thee,
    Nor what is mine shall never do thee good.
    Trust to't, bethink you! I'll not be forsworn!

The boys stop and back away, terrified by their own violence.
Student 1 *grabs the fabric and holds it up in front of* **Student 2**,
shielding his body from the view of the other two boys and he looks

away trying to offer some privacy. **Student 2** *stands and tries to pull his trousers up; it is a physical and emotional effort.* **Student 3** *tries to help but* **Student 2** *does not let him approach. He tries to pull his trousers up again, but he cannot do it.* **Students 3** *and* **4** *slowly approach and pull* **Student 2**'s *trousers up for him. All four embrace.*

All   Is there no pity sitting in the clouds
  That sees into the bottom of my grief?

Student 2 *goes to* **Student 3** *and tries to play the rest of the scene but* **Student 3** *backs away, refusing to go on.*

Student 2 (*as Juliet*)   O sweet my mother, cast me not away,
  Delay this marriage for a month, a week,
  Or if you do not, make the bridal bed
  In that dim monument where Tybalt lies.

Student 2 *hands* **Student 3** *the script, desperate to go on.*
Student 3 *finally takes the script and reads.*

Student 3 (*as Lady Capulet*)
  Talk not to me, for I'll not speak a word.
  Do as thou wilt, for I have done with thee.

Student 3 *exits the scene.* **Student 2** *grabs* **Student 4**.

Student 2 (*as Juliet*)   O God, O Nurse . . . (**Student 4** *does not want to play.*) Nurse . . . Nurse!

  How shall this be prevented?
  My husband is on earth, my faith in heaven.
  How shall that faith return again to earth
  Unless that husband send it me from heaven.
  By leaving earth? Comfort me, cousel me.
  What sayst thou? Hast thou not a word of joy.

Student 4 *has no idea what to do.* **Student 1** *grabs the book and brings it to them, flipping through it.*

Student 1   Faith, here it is.

Student 4
  'Romeo is banish'd, and all the world to nothing

That he dares ne'er come back to challenge you.'

Students 4 and 3 'Or if he do, it needs must be by stealth.'

Student 4 'Then, since the case so stands as now it doth,'

All 'I think it best you married with the County!'

They drop the book shattered. **Student 4** *goes to* **Student 2** *and tries to comfort him.* **Student 2** *pushes him away.* **Student 4** *starts folding the fabric, avoiding eye contact with* **Student 2**.

Student 4 (*as Nurse*) O, he's a lovely gentleman.
Romeo's a dishclout to him. An eagle, madam,
Hath not so green, so quick, so fair an eye
As Paris hath. Beshrew my very heart,
I think you are happy in this second match,
For it excels your first; or, if it did not,
Your first is dead, or 'twere as good he were
As living here and you no use of him.

Student 2 (*as Juliet*) Speakest thou from thy heart?

Student 4 (*as Nurse*)
And from my soul too, else beshrew them both.

Student 2 (*as Juliet*) Amen.

Student 4 (*as Nurse*) What?

Student 2 (*as Juliet*)
Well, thou hast comforted me marvellous much.
Go in, and tell my lady I am gone,
Having displeas'd my father, to Laurence's cell,
To make confession and to be absolv'd.

Student 4 (*as Nurse*) Marry, I will; and this is wisely done.

Student 4 *gives the folded fabric to* **Student 2** *and exits the scene.*

Student 2 (*as Juliet*)
Ancient damnation! O most wicked fiend,
Is it more sin to wish me thus forsworn,
Or to dispraise my lord with that same tongue

Which she hath prais'd him with above compare
So many thousand times? Go, counsellor.
Thou and my bosom henceforth shall be twain.

*We are in **Laurence**'s cell.*

Student 3 (*as Friar*)   O Juliet, I already know thy grief;
It strains me past the compass of my wits.
I hear thou must, and nothing may prorogue it –
On Thursday next be married to this County.

Student 2 (*as Juliet*)
Tell me not, Friar, that thou hear'st of this,
Unless thou tell me how I may prevent it.
If in thy wisdom thou canst give no help,
Do thou but call my resolution wise,
And with this knife –

Student 2 *violently unfurls the fabric.* **Student 4** *slowly picks up
the free end of the fabric and moves in a semi-circle around* **Student 2**,
having the fabric go under **Student 2**'s *arm.*

I'll help it presently.
God join'd my heart and Romeo's, thou our hands;
Therefore, out of thy long-experienc'd time
Give me some present counsel, or behold:

Student 1 *pulls his end of the fabric. The fabric, pulled tautly
between* **Students 1** *and* **2**, *is now a knife.*

'Twixt my extremes and me this bloody knife
Shall play the umpire, arbitrating that
Which the commission of thy years and art
Could to no issue of true honour bring.
Be not so long to speak. I long to die
If what thou speak'st speak not of remedy.

Student 3 (*as Friar*)
Hold, daughter. I do spy a kind of hope
Which craves as desperate an execution
As that is desperate which we would prevent.
If, rather than to marry County Paris,

Thou hast the strength of will to slay thyself,
Then is it likely thou wilt undertake
A thing like death to chide away this shame,
That cop'st with death himself to scape from it.
And if thou dar'st, I'll give thee remedy.

Student 2 (*as Juliet*)

O, bid me leap into a new-made grave,
And hide me with a dead man in his shroud,
And I will do it without fear or doubt,
To live an unstain'd wife to my sweet love.

Student 3 (*as Friar*)

Hold then. Go home, be merry, give consent
To marry Paris. Wednesday is tomorrow;
Tomorrow night look that thou lie alone.
Let not thy Nurse lie with thee in thy chamber.

Student 3 *takes the end of the fabric from* **Student 4**. *Throughout the rest of this speech,* **Student 3** *carefully rolls up the fabric until he gets it away from* **Student 2**.

Take thou this vial, being then in bed,
And this distilling liquor drink thou off;
When presently through all thy veins shall run
A cold and drowsy humour, for no pulse
Shall keep his native progress, but surcease:
Each part depriv'd of supple government
Shall stiff and stark and cold appear, like death,
And in this borrow'd likeness of shrunk death
Thou shalt continue two and forty hours
And then awake as from a pleasant sleep.
Now when the bridegroom in the morning comes
To rouse thee from thy bed, there art thou, dead.
Then as the manner of our country is,
In thy best robes, uncover'd on the bier
Thou shalt be borne to that same ancient vault
Where all the kindred of the Capulets lie.
In the meantime, against thou shalt awake,
Shall Romeo by my letters know our drift

And hither shall he come / and he and I
Will watch thy waking, and that very night
Shall Romeo bear thee hence to Mantua . . .

Student 1   Shall I compare thee to a summer's day?
Thou art more lovely and more temperate.
Rough winds do shake the darling buds of May
And summer's lease hath all too short a date.

Student 3 *hands the fabric to* **Student 2** *who grasps it as the vial.*

Student 2   Romeo? . . . Romeo . . .

Student 1 *comes to* **Student 2**.

Romeo, here's drink.

Student 2 *hands one end of the fabric to* **Student 1**.

I drink to thee!

Student 1 *pulls the fabric and* **Student 2** *falls to the ground. The others fall asleep. Bells ring.* **Students 3** *and* **4** *wake up startled, looking around terrified as if waking from a nightmare. They look at each other relieved.*

Students 3 and 4   Good faith. 'Tis day.

They start laughing and cleaning up the room. **Student 4** *notices* **Student 2**'s *body.*

Student 4 (*as Nurse*)
Alas, alas . . . Help . . . help! My lady's dead . . .
O lamentable day . . .

Student 3 (*as Lady Capulet*)   What is the matter?

Student 4 (*as Nurse*)   Look . . . look! O heavy day . . .
She's dead . . . deceas'd . . . She's dead . . . Alack the
day . . .

Student 3 (*as Lady Capulet*)
Death, that hath ta'en her hence to make me wail
Ties up my tongue and will not let me speak.

*Students 4 and 3 gasp for air. They stop as **Student 1** awakens with a laugh, **Student 2** with a scream, **Student 2** goes and grabs the book, rifling through it as **Student 1** continues.*

Student 1 (*as Romeo*)
    I dreamt my lady came and found me dead –
    Strange dream that gives a dead man leave to think! –
    And breathes such life with kisses in my lips
    That I revive and am an emperor.
    Ah me, how sweet is love itself possess'd
    When but love's shadows are so rich in joy.

*Student 4 approaches him as **Balthazar**.*

Student 1 (*as Romeo*)
    News from Verona! How, now Balthasar,
    Dost thou not bring me letters from the Friar?
    How doth my lady?

Student 4 cannot look at him and turns away.

                  Is my father well?
    How doth my Juliet? That I ask again,
    For nothing can be ill if she be well.

Student 4 (*as Balthazar*)
    Then she is well and nothing can be ill.

*Unable to tell his news, **Student 4** begins to leave. **Student 1** stops him. **Student 4** hands him the book and **Student 1** reads.*

Student 1   'Her body sleeps in Capels' monument,
    And her immortal part with angels lives.'

He cannot believe it.

Student 4 (*as Balthazar*)
    I saw her laid low in her kindred's vault
    And presently took post to tell it you.
    O pardon me for bringing these ill news,
    Since you did leave it for my office, sir.

Student 1 (*as Romeo*)   Is it e'en so?

Student 1 *paces. He throws the book.*

> Then I defy you, stars!
> Thou know'st my lodging. Get me ink and paper,
> And hire posthorses. I will hence tonight.

Student 4 (*as Balthazar*)
> I do beseech you sir, have patience.
> Your looks are pale and wild and do import
> Some misadventure.

Student 1 (*as Romeo*)   Tush, thou art deceiv'd.
> Leave me, and do the thing I bid thee do.
> Hast thou no letters to me from the Friar?

Student 4 (*as Balthazar*)   No, my good lord.

Students 3 *and* **2** *read furiously from the script as* **Friar Laurence** *and* **Friar John**.

Student 3 (*as Friar*)   Friar John.
> Welcome from Mantua. What says Romeo?
> Or, if his mind be writ, give me his letter.

Student 2 (*as Friar John*)
> Going to find a barefoot brother out,
> One of our order, to associate me,
> Here in this city visiting the sick,
> And finding him, the searchers of the town,
> Suspecting that we both were in a house
> Where the infectious pestilence did reign,
> Seal'd up the doors and would not let us forth,
> So that my speed to Mantua there was stay'd.

Student 3 (*as Friar*)   Who bare my letter then to Romeo?

Student 2 (*as Friar John*)   I could not send it
> Nor get a messenger to bring it thee,
> So fearful were they of infection.

They close the script.

Student 3 (*as Friar*)   Unhappy fortune. This may do much danger.

Student 1 (*as Romeo*)   Get thee gone.
  And hire those horses. I'll be with thee straight.

Student 4 *exits the scene.*

  Well, Juliet, I will lie with thee tonight.
  Let's see for means. O mischief thou art swift
  To enter in the thoughts of desperate men.
  I do remember an apothecary.

Students 2, 3 *and* **4** *appear as the* **Apothecary**. **Student 2**
hands the fabric to **Student 1**.

Students 2, 3 and 4 (*spoken in a round*)
  Put this in any liquid thing you will
  And drink it off and if you had the strength
  Of twenty men it would dispatch you straight.

Student 1 (*as Romeo*)
  Come, cordial, and not poison, go with me
  To Juliet's grave, for there must I use thee.

Students 3 *and* **4** *set up the crypt as* **Student 2** *walks centre
stage and lies down as the seemingly dead Juliet.* **Student 1** *prizes
open the crypt.*

Student 1 (*as Romeo*)
  Thou detestable maw, thou womb of death
  Gorg'd with the dearest morsel of the earth,
  Thus I enforce thy rotten jaws to open,
  And in despite I'll cram thee with more food.

Student 1 *enters the crypt.*

  O here lies Juliet, and her beauty makes
  This vault a feasting presence, full of light.
  How oft when men are at the point of death
  Have they been merry! Which their keepers call
  A lightning before death. O how may I
  Call this a lightning?

He kneels next to **Student 2**.

                    O my love, my wife,

Death that hath suck'd the honey of thy breath
Hath had no power yet upon thy beauty.
Thou art not conquer'd. Beauty's ensign yet
Is crimson in thy lips and in thy cheeks,
And Death's pale flag is not advanced there.
Why art thou yet so fair? Shall I believe
That unsubstantial Death is amorous,
And that the lean abhorred monster keeps
Thee here in dark to be his paramour?
For fear of that I still will stay with thee,
And never from this palace of dim night
Depart again. Here, here, will I remain
With worms that are thy chambermaids. O here
Will I set up my everlasting rest
And shake the yoke of inauspicious stars
From this world-wearied flesh. Eyes, look your last.
Arms, take your last embrace! And lips, O you
The doors of breath, seal with a righteous kiss
A dateless bargain to engrossing Death.

As **Student 1** *takes up the fabric,* **Student 4** *moves toward him.*

Come, bitter conduct, come unsavoury guide,
Thou desperate pilot now at once run on
The dashing rocks thy seasick weary bark.
Here's to my love!

Student 4 *takes one end of the fabric and pulls in through*
Student 1's *grasping hand.*

O true apothecary,
Thy drugs are quick.

Student 1 *kisses* **Student 2**.

Thus with a kiss I die.

Student 1 *falls. A long silence. A sound.* **Students 3** *and* **4** *look at each other, terrified.*

Student 4   Fear comes upon me.

Student 3   O, much I fear some ill unthrifty thing.

The two run to **Student 1** *and try to rouse him.*

Student 3   Romeo . . .

Student 1 *does not move.*

Student 4   O, pale . . .

Student 3   Ah what an unkind hour
Is guilty of this lamentable chance?

Student 2 *awakens.*

Student 4   The lady stirs.

He goes and checks the door to make sure no one is coming as
Student 3 *checks* **Student 2**.

Student 2 (*as Juliet*)
O comfortable Friar, where is my lord?
I do remember well where I should be,
And there I am. Where is my Romeo?

Student 3 *takes* **Student 2** *and tries to get him to leave. Another sound.*

Student 4   I hear some noise.

Student 3   Lady, come from that nest
Of death, contagion, and unnatural sleep.
A greater power than we can contradict
Hath thwarted our intents.

As the marching continues, **Student 4** *grabs the clothes and composition books from under the floorboards.*

Student 4   Come, come away.

Student 2 *notices* **Student 1**'s *body.*

Student 3   Thy husband in thy bosom there lies dead,
Come Juliet, come, I'll dispose of thee
Among a sisterhood of holy nuns.

Student 2 *runs to* **Student 1**'s *body.*

Student 4   Stay not to question, for the Watch is coming.

Student 3   Come, go, good Juliet.

Students 3 *and* **4** *grab their uniforms and dress.*

Student 2 *notices the fabric in* **Student 1**'s hand.

Student 2 (*as Juliet*)
What's here? A cup clos'd in my true love's hand?
Poison, I see, hath been his timeless end.

He cannot pull the fabric from **Student 1**'s tight grasp.

O churl. Drunk all, and left no friendly drop
To help me after? I will kiss thy lips.
Haply some poison yet doth hang on them
To make me die with a restorative.

He kisses **Student 1**.

Thy lips are warm!

Students 3 *and* **4** *start marching.*

Student 2 (*as Juliet*)
Yea, noise? Then I'll be brief. O happy dagger.
This is thy sheath.

Student 2 *takes the fabric and wraps it around his chest.*

There rust, and let me die.

Student 3 *takes one end of the fabric and pulls.* **Student 2** *falls across* **Student 1**'s *body. The marching stops. Pause. School bells ring. It is morning. the 'dream' is over.*

Student 3   Now, ere the sun advance his burning eye
The day to cheer, and nights dank dew to dry.

Students 2, 3 *and* **4** *hurriedly put on their ties and sweaters and collect their books. They begin their daily lessons.*

Student 2   Amo, amas, amat, amamus, amatis,
amant . . . (*He repeats through* **Student 1**'s *speech below.*)

Student 3   The business of a man is to govern the world, and the destiny of a woman is to charm and influence it.(*He repeats through* **Student 1**'s *speech below.*)

Student 4   Thou shalt not lie, steal, cheat, kill, lust. (*He repeats through* **Student 1**'s *speech below.*)

Once dressed, they begin marching and start to leave. **Student 1** *runs and grabs the copy of* Romeo and Juliet *and tries to hold his fellow students with his words, then physically as well.*

Student 1   Now it is the time of night
   That the graves, all gaping wide,
   Everyone lets forth his sprite.
   In the churchway paths to glide
   And we fairies, that do run
   By the triple Hecate's team
   From the presence of the sun,
   Following darkness like a dream,
   Now are frolic!
   Now is the time of night . . .
   Now is the time of night . . .
   Now is the time of night . . . !

Student 2 *grabs* **Student 1** *and holds him.*

Student 2   If these shadows have offended,
   Think but this, and all is mended:
   That we have but . . . slumbered here
   While these visions did appear.
   And this weak and idle theme,
   No more yielding but a dream.

Students 2, **3**, *and* **4** *begin to march away.*

Student 1   If we be friends, give me your hands.

Students 2, **3**, *and* **4** *join* **Student 1**. *They clasp hands.*

   A glooming peace this morning with it brings:
   The sun for sorrow will not show his head.
   Go hence to have more talk of these sad things.

Student 1 *takes the copy of R & J and reads from it. It is the most difficult thing he has ever had to do.*

For never was a story of more woe
Than this of Juliet and her Romeo.

He closes the book. Their evening is over. **Students 2**, **3** *and* **4** *march off.* **Student 1** *clutches the book.*

Student 1   I dreamt a dream tonight.
I dreamt . . . I dreamt . . . I dreamt . . .

Lights fade.